CIGAR CHIC: A WOMAN'S PERSPECTIVE

CIGAR CHIC: A WOMAN'S PERSPECTIVE

Tomima Edmark

THE SUMMIT PUBLISHING GROUP
1112 East Copeland Road, Fifth Floor • Arlington, Texas 76011

Printed in the United States of America.

99 98 97 96   5

Library of Congress Cataloging in Publication Data

Edmark, Tomima
    Cigar chic : a woman's perspective / Tomama Edmark.
        p. cm.
    ISBN 1-56530-193-5 (hardcover)
        1. Cigars. 2. Women—Tobacco use. Title.
TS2260.E36 1995
394.1'4—dc20   95-4365
                                                    CIP

Cover Design by David Sims
Book Design by John Baird
Photographs by Truitt Rogers
Photograph pg.65 by Steve Foxall

CONTENTS

ACKNOWLEDGMENTS

My thanks to Dolores Donner and to
Richard L. DiMeola, Marilyn Weber, David Ishii,
Brian O. Ardelean, and Al Cooper
for their invaluable contributions

FOREWORD

I am not writing this book to condone smoking. I am an adult who enjoys smoking cigars and who has made a personal decision to do so. This book is simply an effort to provide information on the subject of cigars for everyone, but particularly for women.

My decision to smoke cigars was not a casual one. I have always been health conscious, have never smoked a cigarette, and have supported the rights of nonsmokers regarding secondhand smoke. I feel that it is unfair, however, to lump cigar smoking into the same category as cigarette smoking for several reasons.

Cigar tobacco is very low in nicotine and acidity when compared to cigarette tobacco. This lower acidity makes it more tolerable to the palate. A cigar produces an alkaline smoke that is stronger and thus is less likely to be inhaled than cigarette smoke, whose higher nicotine content makes its smoke smoother. During the fermentation process of cigar tobacco, chemical changes cause a loss of nicotine. Cigarette tobacco, by contrast, is finely shredded, causing more surface exposure and higher burning temperature. Cigars burn slower and cooler.

Cigar smoking, as a rule, is done in moderation. Most people smoke a cigar after dinner, preferably with a drink. Consequently, moderate cigar smoking has never been lumped with cigarette smoking as unhealthy. The *Journal of the American Medical Association* reports about exposure to secondhand tobacco smoke, "It would take 42.6 eight-hour days (more than eight weeks of work) for an individual to be exposed to the nicotine equivalent in smoking a single cigarette." The impact of being around an occasional cigar, of course, would be even less.

Cigar smokers do not inhale. The flavor of the smoke is enjoyed if held in the mouth—not in the lungs. The strength of cigar smoke also makes it uncomfortable to inhale. Those who do accidentally inhale usually become nauseated and/or dizzy. A 1982 surgeon general's report, *The Health Consequences of Smoking,* offers the following: "… the risk of developing lung cancer for cigar smokers is less than that for cigarette smokers. In contrast with cigarette smokers, most cigar smokers report that they do not inhale the smoke, and as a consequence, the total exposure of the lungs to tobacco smoke remains relatively low." It should not be disregarded, however, that some risk is involved if cigar smoke is inhaled

Finally, Don Shopland, coordinator of the National Cancer Institute, says, "An occasional cigar, one a day, is not too worrisome." That's more than the average cigar usage of five a week.

Of course, abuse of any product can cause health problems, but the cigar, by its nature and price, is not commonly exploited.

Cigars are different than cigarettes in the same way that fine wine is different than soft drinks. Cigars are made from the best tobacco available. Much time and attention is given to selecting the leaves as well as to making the cigar itself. Cigars, like wines, are carefully blended for flavor. Just as a good wine should be sipped and cherished, so should a fine cigar be smoked slowly and appreciated. Cigar etiquette dictates that under no circumstance should secondhand smoke from a cigar float in the direction of an unwilling party.

INTRODUCTION

I smoked my first cigar during a business trip to South America. Returning from a dinner given by one of the embassies in Santiago, Chile, I walked into my hotel lobby and found a curious congregation of twelve other delegates, all men, sitting in a circle puffing away on Cuban H. Upmanns. I was spotted immediately by this fraternal powwow, and one of the members goaded me to join the ritual. Well, having grown up with five brothers, I find a dare hard to turn down, so, in cocktail dress and pearls, I accepted the invitation, to the men's surprise and obvious delight. I have to say that I didn't adore the taste right away, but I instantly understood the pleasure in the ritual—cutting the cigar, holding it, gesturing with it.

I was not married at the time but was just starting to be courted by Stephen, who is now my husband. I told him my experience and discovered that he had been a longtime cigar aficionado. He endeared himself to me in many ways, but particularly by showing me the fine points of selecting, cutting, and smoking a cigar. On the night he proposed, we smoked Romeo y Julietas to celebrate. I saved the stubs and bands and have them framed in a shadow box.

I was now charmed by the cigar. I wanted to know everything about it. I began searching for information about other women who have been enthralled by the cigar's mystique. I found very little. In fact, basic information was hard to come by. The books and articles available were not written for beginners but rather for cigar masters, who were presumed to be men only.

This book is intended to remedy that, to share the basics of cigars: where they came from, how to smoke them, and why so many people enjoy them. Particular attention is given to women and to their participation in, and influence on, cigar smoking. I was surprised by what I found and know that you will be, too. This book does not, however, list and evaluate specific cigars. Other books and magazines do a nice job of that.

Who smokes cigars? The group is eclectic. The entry age has been around thirty-five, with the majority of smokers being between fifty-five and sixty-five. But in recent years the entry age has become younger: mid- to late twenties. Cigar smokers come from all socioeconomic and ethnic backgrounds. However, they all pride themselves on being well-mannered and nonobtrusive in their smoking. Most smoke in private. A small percentage (which is getting larger) smoke in public places, which include smoking clubs and organized smoking events called "smokers." Women cigar smokers, unfortunately, must carry an added burden—the disapproval of nonsmoking women who, ironically, disapprove less of men who smoke cigars. Men, on the other hand, are rarely offended by cigar smokers.

Most cigar smokers don't *have* to smoke, unlike most cigarette smokers. Cigar smokers are not addicts. They are connoisseurs, always looking for the next great cigar. It's an avocation, a hobby. The price of a premium cigar ranges from one to thirty-five dollars, so the cost is self-regulating.

A woman should at least try a cigar. It's one of life's pleasures. If, however, a woman chooses not to smoke cigars, she should certainly know something about them. There is a lot to be discovered about a man by the way he selects and smokes his cigar. Smoking cigars can also be a great couple activity. It brings back the art of conversation. It also encourages closeness and sharing.

Stephen and I spend many evenings a week smoking together. Such evenings are uninterrupted times for us when we can experiment with different kinds of cigars, talk, unwind, and—most important to us—reduce stress. We have a "smoke room" with two large leather chairs and all our cigar paraphernalia (humidors, cutters, smoking hats, lighters, matches, etc.) overlooking our pool. Large windows and a strong air purifier assure that the room and our house in general never suffer from stale smoke odors. Most of the time, we walk the dogs or float our cognac snifters in the spa while we smoke. On fall evenings, we practice our fly casting over the pool with cigars hanging from our mouths (we know, we know—bad form).

We have a journal to keep track of all the different kinds of cigars we smoke while experimenting. We save the bands and put them in the journal along with our opinions. Recently we tried Casa Blanca Robustos, made famous by Robert DeNiro in the movie *Cape Fear*. Stephen's had a nice draw, burned very evenly. The ash stayed on the entire smoke. Mine, on the other hand, was rolled too loosely, thus drawing on it was like sucking on a garden hose.

I smoke cigars because I enjoy them. The taste and smoke are pleasant. The fact that my husband also smokes cigars makes the hobby all the more pleasurable. I like large cigars such as the Churchill size. I don't like the "little ones" that women are usually offered. My advice to women (and men) who want to experiment is: If you're going to smoke cigars, don't be afraid of the big ones. They're actually milder. And most important, don't forget: Don't *inhale!*

And now, ladies—to echo King Edward VII—you may smoke.

CHAPTER 1

HISTORY

A New Leaf

No one knows for sure who first dried and rolled together tobacco leaves and then smoked them. Perhaps a native island woman wrapped food in a tobacco leaf before placing it in the cooking fire, and the resultant flavor piqued her interest. Mystery shrouds what was probably a less than auspicious beginning of what we now know as the cigar.

The Mayan culture first documented the practice of smoking dried tobacco more than two thousand years ago; it is not recorded whether or not Mayan women participated in this activity, but it is highly probable. When the Mayan culture broke up, the scattering tribes carried tobacco to other locations in the Americas.

During Columbus's voyage of 1492 his sailors discovered the Arawak Indians of the Caribbean smoking loosely rolled cigars. These sailors were the first white men to see a cigar or tobacco in any form. Later, Spanish conquistadores, returning from the interior of Peru, were the first to report seeing women smoking cigars.

The cigars that the Central American Indians smoked at that time were not at all like modern cigars. They were made of crude tobacco rolled and wrapped in a sheath from palm trees or a strip of maize. The tobacco inside was uncured and, in many cases, acrid because the Indians steeped it in seawater.

Rites and Rituals

Tobacco is native to the Americas, and the first cigars were abnormally large—four hands high—and were carried around lighted most of the day. In some parts of Central and South America, these huge cigars were used in religious dance rituals. As the cigars were smoked, the smoke was blown on warriors to invoke courage.

At least a thousand years before Columbus anchored at what is now known as the island of San Salvador in the Bahamas, Indians were smoking rolled tobacco. They, too, used tobacco in their religious ceremonies and believed it to have healing properties.

In Search of Gold

We're all familiar with the first voyage of Columbus. Perhaps that odyssey should be called "The Gold Rush of '92."

After much cajoling by Columbus, Spain's Queen Isabella finally was convinced to finance his expedition to search for the new world. In reality, Isabella's interest centered more on expanding Spain's influence and filling her coffers with gold than on finding what probably seemed to her to be a place of mere imagination. Little did anyone realize that the "gold" that Columbus would find grew from lush, green plants among orchids, towering palms, and mango trees.

Rodrigo de Xeves, an explorer on Columbus's ship, first reported the phenomenon of smoking. Columbus had sent him inland to find gold. Instead, he returned with news of people who were "drinking smoke," of "chimney men" who carried a brown tube burning at one end. They drank from the other end, and smoke came out.

In his *Journal of the First Voyage* (October 6, 1492), Columbus wrote, "The two Christians met on the way many people who were going to their towns, women and men, with a firebrand in the hand… "

The Spanish Seed

Exploration and conquest gave the Spanish and the Portuguese a stronghold in Central and South America, so England and other northern European countries explored the northern Americas. This separation had a profound influence on the history of smoking habits.

Tobacco belonged to the Spaniards. From places such as Cuba—which came under Spanish rule in 1515—they transported the tiny seeds to Europe. The Spaniards and the Portuguese smoked tobacco in the form of the cigar, whereas northern Europeans used the pipe. The cigar attained widespread popularity north of the Pyrenees only in the nineteenth century—more than three hundred years after the cigar had been perfected in Seville.

Jean Nicot, the French ambassador to Portugal and Spain, gave the tobacco plant its generic name of *nicotine* and was the first man to take the plant north of the Pyrenees in 1559. He thought so highly of tobacco's medicinal properties that he sent seeds from Portugal back to Catherine de' Medici (wife of Henry II of France) to cure her migraine headaches. Her influence caused tobacco to be grown in many French botanical gardens to be made into medicinal snuff.

The Spaniards were the first Europeans to cultivate substantial amounts of tobacco in Spain, in Cuba, and elsewhere in the New World, and soon large plantations flourished. Spanish influence helped to improve the configuration of the cigar and is the reason why many cigars have Spanish names today.

In one improved version of the cigar, tobacco was rolled in a tobacco leaf with a straw inserted in the middle. By the mid-sixteenth century, cigars with smaller shapes appeared. Some had wrappers of bark or vegetable leaves.

Spain's monopoly on tobacco and cigars provided more wealth for the country than did the elusive gold that the conquistadores diligently sought. Tobacco growing and cigar smoking by the Spanish raised the social level of those who smoked cigars, and it was common for Spanish countesses and duchesses to smoke cigars just as their husbands did. Not until the early nineteenth century was the Spanish monopoly finally broken.

English Élan

Probably not many of us have had a gentleman friend spread his topcoat across a mud puddle to ensure our dry crossing, but Sir Walter Raleigh, that paradigm of chivalry, not only knew how to treat a woman—and how to write poetry—but he also probably was responsible for introducing tobacco and the new fashion of smoking to Britain.

Raleigh's colony in Virginia had tobacco plantations. He also imported tobacco into the colonies. (Tragically, tobacco eventually wed the tobacco-producing colonies to the slave system of labor.) With his fortune so tied up in tobacco, Raleigh did everything he could to encourage smoking in England. In 1585, he sent Ralph Lane, the governor of his colony, to England with tobacco plants and seed.

Sir Walter was one of the first smokers in England and began the popularization of smoking there. In fact, he enjoyed a great vogue in London when he puffed on his pipe before Queen Elizabeth. This strange practice of inhaling smoke was so intriguing that two Indians were brought from Virginia to London to demonstrate it.

Today the Austrian Tobacco Museum in Vienna displays Raleigh's personal chest, in which he transported tobacco across the ocean, near a cabinet of pre-Castro Cuban cigars.

England's men of fashion switched from smoking pipes to smoking cigars for several reasons: They found it novel, they considered cigars more genteel than pipes, and cigars were sufficiently expensive to remain a rich man's luxury.

Cigars from Cuba are thought to have arrived in the American colonies around 1762 because the British invaded Cuba in that year and briefly occupied it. Although he was not British, Israel Putnam, an officer in the British army serving in Cuba, returned to his home in Connecticut with Cuban cigars and tobacco. Putnam later became an American general during the Revolutionary War.

In northern Europe it's not clear what changed interest from pipe smoking to cigar smoking, but in 1779 the papal government in Rome granted a five-year concession to Peter Wendler, a German painter living in Italy, to manufacture cigars. Ten years later, cigar factories were in Germany and France. Northern Europe was now awakened to the joy of the cigar.

Jumping on the Bandwagon

Well before 1779 tobacco production and consumption had already circled the globe, and it was found in Russia, the Philippines, Virginia, Java, India, and Ceylon—it was snuffed, smoked, and chewed. In the American colonies around Chesapeake Bay it was a medium of exchange— used to pay salaries, taxes, and rent.

Although cigar smoking in America didn't take off until the time of the Civil War, the first factory to make handrolled cigars in the States was opened in Connecticut in 1810. Hartford became the home of many cigar factories, and cigar smoking quickly became popular. Cigar smoking also flourished in the Conestoga region of Pennsylvania. A reduction in the tobacco tax in the 1870s made cigars even more popular and widely available. In the mid-nineteenth century, the cigar box and the cigar band were introduced because brand and

Cigar Store Indians

Nineteenth-century America was a melting pot that lacked a common language as a stirring spoon, so the cigar store Indian was vital for cigar store business. This visual sign was a stand-in for written signposts. The Indian was used as a symbol because those in Central America introduced Columbus to tobacco, but cigar store Indians are not accurate representations of any tribe because they were crafted by artisans who had never actually seen an Indian—North or Central American.

Today, cigar store Indians are virtually extinct—only around two thousand remain. But that's enough to keep the Society for the Preservation of the Wooden Indian alive and well.

America's most impressive collection of wooden Indians is on display at the New York offices of General Cigar and Tobacco Company.

size variations were becoming important and because counterfeit cigars were becoming a major problem. By the latter part of the nineteenth century, cigars had become a status symbol.

During this time the practice of reading to workers in cigar factories began in Cuba. Such reading educated the workers and alleviated their boredom. Workers paid for the readers out of their own wages. Cuban cigar rollers became well-versed in the classics because the readers read primarily from literary works.

CHAPTER 2

THE FEMALE INFLUENCE

Ladies of Spain

Women have a legendary association with cigars. The first tobacco factory in Europe was established in Spain in 1620. During the seventeenth century, women were employed to make cigars in the factories in Seville and were the inspiration for the images of many French writers.

Prosper Merimee's book *Carmen* was conceived by observing such women and was later adapted to the opera of the same name, in which Carmen brazenly smokes cigars in the town square.

Of early female tobacco handlers in Spain, Pierre Louys wrote, "The prudes wear a blouse, but most of the girls work with breasts exposed, clad only in a simple cloth skirt tucked up around their thighs. Some of the bodies, it is true, were unattractive, but all were interesting, and many were most beautiful, with full bosoms and clear shining skin." Mothers took their babies to work with them; sleeping babies lay beside working mothers.

A woman was employed in a cigar factory in Havana for the first time in 1878. She was European. But not until the 1960s were women allowed to roll cigars in Cuban factories—a craft that had been for men only. Before then, women's tasks had been restricted to sorting tobacco leaves. Women had not been allowed to roll cigars partly because of religious reasons, partly because of union rules. The women often sorted leaves on their thighs, giving rise to the famous myth that Cuban cigars were rolled on the thighs of beautiful Cuban maidens.

In fourteenth-century Aztec culture, tobacco gourds and pouches were the insignia of women doctors and midwives. During the early 1600s, European doctors believed that there was a link between women's health and tobacco. Thus they prescribed handrolled tobacco—"cigars"—for their women patients to cure headaches, toothaches, and runny noses. In Latin America, the use of cigars by women in their homespun healing rituals is common.

Feminine Indulgences

Equal numbers of men and women in Europe and America smoked cigars during the eighteenth century. Through the 1830s, American women smoked frequently. In 1846 Charles Dickens met an American woman and her daughter in Germany: After dinner, both joined him in smoking cigars.

Nineteenth-century European women of society showed increased enthusiasm for cigar smoking but indulged behind the closed doors of Turkish baths for women or in their boudoirs.

That old antagonist, social pressure, had its way with women cigar smokers of the late nineteenth and early twentieth centuries, although Latin American women did not suffer the stigma as much as did American and European women.

To avoid the social reproach aimed at women who smoked cigars, women who rolled cigars in factories in Florida would cut cigars and reroll the tobacco in cigarette papers and hold them together with a hairpin. A nice little touch, and proof once again of feminine ingenuity.

Women who did smoke openly during this era generally preferred "queens"—cigars of diminutive size, some of which had "small straw mouthpieces."

If women didn't smoke cigars, they certainly bought them for their husbands. This was true all the way to the top: The queen of Spain spent $1,000 on cigars in Havana for her consort-husband, Don Francisco de Asii.

In 1920 the American tobacco industry aimed its advertising at encouraging women to smoke cigarettes. Such advertising made cigar smoking seem cumbersome and time consuming. Later advertising by Muriel cigars is well remembered: Edie Adams, followed by Susan Anton in 1970, coquettishly mouthed, "Pick me up and smoke me sometime."

In Berlin during the 1920s there were women's cigar-smoking clubs made up of artists, writers, club owners, and demimondaines (women who have lost social standing because of sexual promiscuity). The clubs mushroomed. They were places for progressive women to get together and network, socialize, and exert their power.

Such clubs also sprang up in New York, Chicago, and other major cities in the United States, but little evidence of them exists today. They functioned behind a smoky shroud of secrecy.

No such secrecy for Bonnie Parker. Parker, of the infamous Bonnie and Clyde, was a "sometimes" poet and bank robber. As she and Clyde wreaked havoc across the Southwest during the Depression, she smoked cigars—perhaps an unexpected and elegant touch for one of such notoriety.

"A Rose by Any Other Name"

Shakespeare's famous quote means that no matter what you call something, the substance of it remains the same. Shakespeare wasn't the only one to have a way with words. Gertrude Stein (1874–1946) was known for having an acerbic wit and for being a contemporary of Hemingway, Fitzgerald, and other interesting people. She smoked cigars while holding court at her famous literary salon. This modernist grande dame had something to say about the fragrant flower as well: A "rose is a rose is a rose."

What's in a name?

Natives of North, Central, and South America have called tobacco by many names: *cohiba, petum, uppowoc.* No matter what the plant is called, the nicotine in tobacco is actually a liquid that, when extracted from the leaf, is used in insecticides.

What's in a name, indeed?

It seems appropriate to mention here another literary contemporary of Stein—New England biographer and poet Amy Lowell (1874–1925). Lowell defied convention in the early 1900s by smoking cigars and cursing in public. She smoked Manila cigars made in the Philippines and became so addicted to Filipino cigars that, when she realized that World War I was imminent, she bought ten thousand Manilas. It is said that Lowell—who was barely five feet tall and weighed 250 pounds—once caused quite a stir when she smoked a cigar during a visit to Harvard: Her brother, Abbott Lawrence Lowell, was Harvard's president at the time.

Bryther Ellerman, the English benefactress of James Joyce, the Sitwells, and later Dylan Thomas, was another notorious cigar-smoking lady earlier in this century.

Sidonie Gabrielle Colette (1873–1954), a French novelist commonly referred to as just "Colette," was rumored to have smoked cigars in bed. She wrote *Gigi* and included in it a scene in which Gigi was taught the importance of a man's cigar and how to select one.

How about dessert? Specifically, peach Melba (followed by a good cigar, of course). Nellie Melba, an Australian *coloratura* soprano, invented the scrumptious confection bearing her name. Actually, her real name was Mrs. Armstrong, but she took her stage name from Melbourne and her vocal strength from smoking cigars.

The owner of La Africana cigar factory in Cuba (the first factory to employ a woman in 1878) sent Nellie the factory's choicest cigars. She loved to blow smoke rings and enjoyed a Havana before every performance.

Other women of this period who smoked in public included: Marie d'Agoult, who wrote under the name of "Daniel Stern" and was the mother of two daughters by composer Franz Liszt; the French animal painter Rosa Bonheur; and the princess of Metternich.

More Name-Dropping

Lillian Russell, a famous American actress, reportedly smoked five hundred three-inch, corona-shaped cigars a month. The manufacturers, grateful for her contribution of charm to the industry, immortalized her on many early lithographs.

More recently, Lucille Ball smoked cigarillos.

In *The Seven Year Itch*, Marilyn Monroe offers a theory about why women weren't smoking cigars: "At the club we had this girl: She smoked nothing but cigars.... Personally, I think she only did it to make herself look older."

Annie Oakley puffed on cheroots to calm her nerves before and after her amazing trick-shooting exhibitions.

The matriarch of the aristocratic Orford family of England chain-smoked black cigars in her elegant salon from 10 P.M. to 2 A.M., much to the consternation of her family and London society in the late nineteenth century.

Singer Cyndi Lauper, whose most famous song is *Girls Just Want to Have Fun,* smokes cigars with men occasionally to prove that she's "just one of the guys."

And that "Material Girl," Madonna, smoked a cigar (her language was smokin', too) during her much-publicized and maligned appearance on "The Late Show with David Letterman" in March 1994.

Scarlet Empresses

Not many of us have color hallmarks that immediately identify us. But some do.

Sophia Frederika of Anholt-serbest, Germany, visited the United States during 1992 and 1993. Actually, she's better known as Catherine the Great (1729–1796), and, of course, she didn't really visit the United States during that time, but an exhibit about her life did.

From her gold-encrusted coach to the fabulous gowns she wore, from her magnificent memorabilia to the written capsulizations of her historic reign, one quickly grasped an impression of this determined and powerful woman. Nowhere in the exhibit, however, was there any evidence of her otherwise well-documented cigar smoking. Catherine is credited with being the first to put a band around a cigar. She requested that a silk band be wrapped around her cigars so that her fingers wouldn't be soiled with tobacco stains.

Catherine reigned as empress of Russia from 1762, when she deposed her husband, Czar Peter III, until her death.

In 1934 Joseph von Sternberg directed the movie *The Scarlet Empress,* which is about Catherine the Great. Marlene Dietrich portrayed her. Dietrich was often seen smoking cigars in films—a habit that she picked up in the cigar clubs of Berlin. In the 1930s she shocked the fashion world by wearing "men's clothing" long before pants and ties were part of women's attire.

Novelist George Sand (1804–1876) also was ahead of her time and may have been the trendsetter for women wearing trousers, trench coats, and neckties as she "cigared" in Paris. She was a strong advocate of women's rights. Wearing men's clothing and smoking cigars—sometimes seven a day—were part of her rebellious lifestyle.

Her real name was Amandine-Aurore-Lucie Dupin, Baronne Dudevant, but she chose a man's name for her work because women weren't published in her day. She had a nine-year liaison with composer Frédéric Chopin four years after breaking up with poet-playwright Alfred de Musset, who had taken to drinking because of his inability to reconcile with her. Both men were six years younger than Sand.

Today her name is perpetuated by the largest women's cigar-smoking society: the George Sand Society, founded in Santa Monica, California, in 1992. The contact there is Kimberly Shaw (310) 394-8667. The New York contact is Tammy Meltzer (212) 757-7610.

Oscars and Stogies

Can we ever forget Thomas Harris's chilling story of Dr. Hannibal Lecter in *The Silence of the Lambs*? Jodie Foster's brilliant portrayal of his nemesis Clarice Starling in the movie adaptation won her an Oscar for best actress. Perhaps when she smokes her occasional cigar, she is one of many who subscribes to the assertion of Christopher J. Steffen, vice chairman of Citicorp, that cigars are "cerebral enhancers."

The story of Whoopi Goldberg's rise to success is also familiar. Another up-by-the-bootstraps climb of a determined and talented woman. She has been smoking cigars since she was a teenager. She'd smoke a cheap cheroot "far away from the radar of my mother."

She's a pro at lighting up, expertly putting a match to a Davidoff, one of her favorite cigars: She prefers punching a hole in the end to snipping. She has been known to use a cigar as a prop, like George Burns, or to flick it like Groucho Marx, then hold it between her upper lip and nose, imitating his mustache. She likes to smoke unhurriedly, finding it comforting and therapeutic.

When the Smoke Clears

It's true that "sometimes a cigar is just a cigar," but the perception changes when women get involved. Not until the latter part of the twentieth century was it again common to see women publicly smoking cigars in the United States. Now, in addition to smoking them, women develop and market cigar accessories, design illustrations for cigar boxes and ashtrays, and a few women own and market their own lines of cigars.

Twenty years ago, if women smoked cigars it very likely was clandestinely for most of them. Only the brave of heart shared this brazen act with their families, and on occasion, with their closest friends. And always discreetly. It's common to hear stories about women—who grew up around and worked with tobacco—whose children or grandchildren would discover them smoking cigars, some of which they rolled themselves.

No need for such secrecy anymore!

As we anticipate the twenty-first century, it's not unusual for women from varied walks of life to smoke cigars in restaurants, at smoking clubs once primarily the domain of men, with colleagues, at the specially organized events called "smokers," and with spouses or other family members.

Grandmothers and mothers are introducing their offspring—male and female—to the mystique, the romance, the pleasure of cigar smoking—an intimacy once shared mostly by grandfathers, fathers, and sons.

Gender specificity is disappearing. As women are becoming more knowledgeable and authoritative about smoking and purchasing cigars, men are welcoming them to the fold. Men are beginning to appreciate the special bonding that can occur when they share and savor the cigar-smoking experience with a special woman. Some men prefer that their wives choose their cigars for them; the purchasing is part of the ritual as well. In fact, to honor this growing influence of women, two cigars have been named the "Estelle" and the "Lena."

Cigar smoking for men has long been a ritual to cel-ebrate births, birthdays, and accomplishments, to enhance political images and backroom caucuses, and to cement relationships while sitting in a comfortable chair and having a chat. Women also are now smoking cigars while they participate in these events.

Kipling wrote in *The Betrothed:* "And a woman is only a woman, but a good cigar is a smoke." A rather pompous statement, but put the two together, and it's a powerful combination.

And more and more it's happening. Of the six to eight million cigar smokers in the United States, the Cigar Association of America estimates that one-tenth of 1 percent are women. In 1995 the magazine *Cigar Aficionado* reported, "The increase in cigar-smoking is due to younger men discovering cigars for the first time, veteran smokers experimenting with a wider variety of brands, and women starting to smoke." Cigar smoking is back from a long exile.

CHAPTER 3

WHAT IS A CIGAR?

Defining Delight

To define something is to consider and then explain its essential qualities. Mark Twain remarked, "No one can tell me what *is* a good cigar—for me. I am the only judge… there are no standards—no *real* standards. Each man's preference is the only standard for him, the only one which he can accept, the only one which can command him."

From a woman's point of view, George Sand had this opinion: "The cigar is the perfect complement to an elegant lifestyle." Those who love cigars seem nearly to attribute personality traits to the other partner in this love affair. And if it's not a love affair, it's certainly a special friendship.

English author William Makepeace Thackeray spoke of this relationship: "I vow and believe that the cigar has been one of the greatest creature comforts of my life—a kind companion, a gentle stimulant, an amicable anodyne, a cementer of friendship… " Certainly cigar smokers have strong emotions about their cigars.

Let's define the cigar by beginning with some basics. The cigar has a body with two ends. The end that is lighted is called the *tuck* or *foot*. The end that goes into your mouth is called the *head*. Many times the cigar will have around it a ring of paper called the *band*. This band identifies the cigar and also helps the smoker to know which end is which because the band is always positioned closer to the head.

A cigar is made of 100 percent tobacco, with the exception of some lower-quality, machine-made cigars. Every premium cigar is constructed with three components: the filler, the binder, and the wrapper. The filler tobacco is the core of the cigar and represents the bulk of its mass. The binder is a tobacco leaf wrapped around the filler to hold it together. The wrapper is the outer covering leaf of the cigar.

A cigar is like a chimney: It must be built or rolled so that its body is in one piece and tight enough to avoid any leaks or perforations. Any holes in the body will cause a loss of smoke and render the cigar unsmokable. The tuck end of the cigar is the chimney pot. Therefore, think of the cigar as a horizontal chimney.

Ah, but the cigar is more than a humble chimney. It is the aristocrat of tobaccos, the smoke of kings—and queens—statesmen, and ambassadors. It is also considered the smoke of democracy and of the common man. It is the smoke of fellowship, political conferences, rejoicing and gatherings, weddings, expectant fathers, special occasions, windfalls, celebrations.

As for the origin of the word for this versatile pleasure, there are several theories about *cigar*. The word could have come:

1. from *cigarro*—male cicadas are called that in southern Spain, where these insects are as big as cigars, with thick, long wings and a dark brown color. Early cigars looked like cicadas made out of paper.
2. from *cigarelle,* Spanish for "garden" (Spanish noblemen grew tobacco in their gardens)
3. from *sik'ar,* Mayan for "smoking" or
4. most likely from the Spanish *cigarrer,* meaning "to roll."

Take your choice.

From Seeds to Smoke

Tobacco growers around the world speak with great passion about growing tobacco for cigars. Tobacco, like corn, is one of those plants that has been domesticated by man. Left to grow in the wild, it would not generate the same quality and quantity of leaf.

Tobacco seeds are minuscule: More than one hundred thousand can fit in a thimble. The most flavorful tobacco grows best in tropical climates. The growing season begins at the end of the rainy season when seedlings that have been raised in a nursery called a *semillero* are planted in special fields that have been sterilized to be free of insects and fungi. So great is the need to keep this environment sterile that the *veguero* (the person who monitors the planting and harvesting) must wear different shoes and clothes, wash his or her hands before entering, and sometimes wear a mask.

When the plant is six inches high it is transferred to the field, where it remains another two months, reaching six to ten feet in height and yielding, at harvest, sixteen to eighteen leaves suitable for cigars. For tobacco grown as wrappers, the fields may be covered with tents made of cheesecloth to block the sunlight. These fields are called *tapados*.

The entire cycle of a cigar plant, from transplanted seedlings to the end of harvesting, takes approximately ninety days. The soil is prepared for planting at the end of April. Mid-September is seed-sowing time. A fortnight later, the first plants are bedded out. Beginning in October, the real planting begins. There's a period of ninety days to reach maturity for wrappers, forty-five to seventy days for filler and binder. Each plant is examined an average of 170 times. It's a very labor-intensive process. After the harvest come more than two hundred manipulations of the leaves, from the original sorting to the boxing of the cigars.

"Double, Double Toil and Trouble..."

The three witches in Shakespeare's *Macbeth* made quite a project out of blending their infamous stew, stirring in bits of newt and frog—you know the story. Making a cigar is, likewise, a complicated process, but it contains only one ingredient—tobacco. The art of making a cigar is the blending of different tobaccos in a suitable wrapper leaf so that the cigar is mild-, medium-, or full-flavored and burns well.

The cigar is not just a roll of tobacco leaf. Frequently it is a blend of tobaccos from different areas of the world. Two exceptions are Mexico and Cuba, where all tobacco comes from their individual countries.

Stirring the Pot

No dabs of newt or dollops of frog are used to make cigars, of course, but all three leaves that make up a cigar do have to go through a complete curing and fermentation process. This process removes chlorophyll and ammonia from the leaves and takes the "bite" out of the tobacco and allows it to burn more evenly. Layer upon layer of tobacco leaves are stacked on pallets, to impressive heights, in large, temperature-controlled warehouses to begin the fermentation process. These stacks of leaves are called "bulks."

During fermentation, the centers of bulks reach temperatures between 115 and 130 degrees Fahrenheit. They then are turned inside out, and the heat buildup (fermentation) begins again. These turns are called "sweats" in the trade. "Sweating" causes emission of nitrogen compounds and other chemical compounds, thus reducing the nicotine, acid, and tar content. The heavier the concentration of gum in the tobacco, the longer the fermentation process.

Fermentation, however, is not an exact science. Bulks vary in size between growers, and sweats are stopped at various temperatures, depending on the traditions or whims of the growers and packers.

When the heat levels off, fermentation is complete: It can take four to eight turns before this happens, and the total process occurs within six to twelve months with some leaves, eighteen to thirty-six months with others. Over-fermentation ruins the leaf, causing it to become "spent" and to lose its flavor and aroma. On the other hand, if the fermentation is cut short, the leaf is still raw, will be very bitter and won't burn properly.

Fermentation helps to assure uniformity in the cigar tobacco and makes it more palatable than cigarette tobacco.

Other factors that determine strength of flavor are the leaf's position on the plant from which it was picked, the soil, and its geographic location. The size of the cigar also affects its strength. Short, thin cigars make for a stronger smoke; large, thick cigars burn slower, thus cooler and milder. The color of the wrapper is *not* an indicator of a cigar's strength, contrary to what many assume.

Fermentation

Growers know when the fermentation process is complete—the tobacco no longer gets hot. If the tobacco in a cigar that you smoke has not been fermented enough, the telltale signs are "cotton mouth," heartburn, and harshness or bitterness on tongue, lips, and in the mouth the next morning. Also, the cigar keeps going out easily.

After fermentation, further aging in bales helps to settle the leaf and to enhance flavor and burning quality. The tobacco leaves in inferior cigars have not been aged properly. Although some say that fermentation continues until the cigar is smoked, fermentation actually ends after the tobacco is made into a cigar.

If proper procedures of fermentation, maturation, and handling are not strictly followed, the quality of the cigar will suffer greatly.

Fill 'er Up

Selecting the proper "filler" to put into a cigar is just as important as selecting the proper gas to put into a car— neither will work if it's not done right. The filler is the core of the cigar. It can consist of leaves of a specific type or a blend of several tobaccos. If filler is a whole leaf or uncut leaves running the length of the cigar, it's called "long filler." Small, chopped pieces are called "short filler."

Long filler has a denser and more evenly structured body, and less surface is exposed to the flame, so

the cigar will smoke slower, cooler, and milder than will a cigar made with short filler. The ash will be longer, too.

Most short-filler cigars are machine made, and many short-filler, mass-market cigars will have the head filled with stem stripped from premium cigar tobacco. Short filler tends to make a cigar less stable, particularly in the head, where it goes into your mouth. The stem stabilizes the head of short-filler cigars and feels better in the mouth. This is a common industry practice.

When a leaf for filler is stripped from the tobacco plant, it is left in one piece. After the stem is taken out, the leaf looks like the underside of a frog. This process is called "frog stripping" and is done for premium cigars.

Filler is three to four separate leaves pleated by hand along their length to allow a passage through which smoke can be drawn when the cigar is lit. This can be properly achieved constantly only by hand and is the primary reason why machine-made cigars have a less satisfactory draw. If you cut a cigar down its length with a razor, the filler leaves would resemble the folds of a fan. Filler leaves are matured seven months to three years.

If a cigar is underfilled—made by skimping on the number of leaves in the filler—it will draw easily, which is a benefit, but it will also burn hot and harsh. Too many air pockets cause a fast, uneven burn that will not hold the ash.

An overfilled cigar is said to be "plugged"—hard or even impossible to draw. A plugged cigar is the biggest complaint of cigar smokers. A hard-to-draw cigar gives a much lower volume of smoke, thus less taste, less aroma, but more frustration.

In a Bind

Ordinarily, people try to avoid getting into a "bind," but not so cigars. In fact, for cigars it's essential. The "binder" is the leaf that is used to wrap and hold the filler. It gives the cigar its shape. Binder leaf is chosen for flavor, aroma, burning qualities, and ash-holding qualities. Unlike filler, binder is half a tobacco leaf.

Filler tobacco held together with a binder leaf is called a *bunch*. When a bunch is being made for a cigar, the tips of the tobacco leaves are always put at the tuck (foot) end because the tips have the most flavor—hence the phrase "tip to tuck."

You Can Judge a Wrap

Unlike a book—which we're told not to judge by its cover—a cigar can be judged by its cover. The cover is called the "wrapper"—the outer leaf of the cigar. It is the finest, most delicate, most expensive leaf used in the cigar. It is thin, silky, flawless, with small or no veins. It is almost transparent, tears easily, and can account for 25 to 50 percent of the cigar's flavor.

The wrapper is what guarantees that the cigar burns. Any damage to the wrapper—being cut, pierced by an insect, or having its band carelessly removed—is a wound that won't heal. The cigar then draws poorly, and both smoke and breath from the smoker will leak out.

The quality of a wrapper leaf is crucial in any cigar. Historically, the best wrapper leaves came from Cuba's El Corojo plantation in the famous Vuelta Abajo area of the Pinar del Rio province. They are shade grown, meaning that they are grown under shade made of cheesecloth to produce a lighter color. The plantation, run by the Cuban government, covers 395 acres and employs six hundred people. Today there are many excellent leaves from other parts of the world.

A single wrapper leaf is cut down the middle and wraps two cigars. Each side of the leaf is rolled around the "bunch" in such a way that the veins run down the cigar with a slow turn. On a right-handed cigar—*derecho*—the veins of the wrapper run on the right side; on the *zurdo*—left-handed cigar—the veins run on the left side. This type of cigar is said to be the quickest on the draw. However, cigars are not sorted in this way, so a box will contain both *derecho* and *zurdo* cigars. It takes a keen eye to distinguish the difference.

Generally, women are more concerned about appearance than are men, and this concern certainly pays off when selecting cigars. So you'll be pleased to know that the condition and quality of the wrapper leaf are critical to the attractive appearance and performance of a cigar as well as to its aroma and flavor.

Wrapper-leaf tobacco, as mentioned earlier, can be grown under cheesecloth (or muslin) or directly under the sun. Either way, it is fermented separately from other leaves to ensure that it is smooth and not too oily and has a subtle bouquet. It must mature for twelve to eighteen months—the longer, the better. The leaf must be soft and pliable to be easy to handle and roll. When tobacco workers strip the leaves from the stems for wrapper and binder leaves, they create two halves at the same time.

Under Cover?

There are three types of leaves on a tobacco plant:

Volado—leaves from the bottom of the plant. The mildest tasting of the leaves; they add bulk and improve burning qualities.

Seco—middle leaves; lighter in color. They are medium flavored, and a plant has more of this type of leaf than any other.

Ligero—leaves from the top of the plant. These have the thickest texture and the greatest concentration of flavor and aroma.

A cigar usually has a blend of all three types of leaves in varying proportions. More *ligero* produces a stronger-tasting cigar. A cigar made of only *seco* would be like a pizza with no toppings. Wrapper leaves usually come from the middle leaves. The best wrappers are grown under shade: This keeps the leaves from becoming too dark and oily and helps them to remain smooth without overdeveloped veins.

For color-conscious women—or men—there are more than fifty shades of wrappers from which to choose. There are too many to mention, but being familiar with the preceding classifications helps. The darker the wrappers, the sweeter the flavor, as with a ripening banana.

It's a Wrap

Finally, the wrapper leaf is rolled over the bunch and kept in place with a tiny drop of colorless and flavorless tragacanth vegetable gum called *goma*. The end of the cigar is capped in several ways:

- It is closed by twisting the end of the wrapper—called "curly head."

- A small, round piece of wrapper leaf the size of a coin is cut out and formed, then stuck in place.
- It is trimmed with a "finished head" cap (see Glossary).

Some non-premium cigars are not capped at all, but instead are given a guillotine end.

Cameroon Decline

Outstanding though it has been, the Cameroon wrapper is now almost impossible to get. The country is underdeveloped, so the tobacco being grown is generally of poor quality now, and many manufacturers have decided that they can no longer count on quantity and quality from Cameroon. To replace Cameroon wrappers, some companies are trying to grow their own wrappers in the Dominican Republic or are buying Indonesian wrapper tobacco, which is actually as good if not better.

Wrappers vary in origin. Cameroon wrappers from Africa are traded almost exclusively through the Meerapfel family in Belgium. From Connecticut comes the Connecticut shade wrapper. And the A. Fuente family is developing a shade wrapper in the Dominican Republic. These are all outstanding wrappers. Brazil, Sumatra, Ecuador, Nicaragua, Honduras, Indonesia, Mexico and Cuba also grow wrapper tobacco.

Green *candela* wrappers were used on 90 percent of the cigars made in the United States before the Cuban embargo. Today less than 2 percent of the cigar market uses *candela* wrappers.

Bands of Gold

Cigar bands have a lore of their own. According to Sydney Clark, author of *All the Best in Cuba*, "cigar bands have a curiously feminine origin." They were first made in Havana to enable high-born Spanish ladies to smoke cigars without bringing their dainty fingers into contact with the weed. However, another theory is that bands were invented to distinguish authentic cigars from counterfeits. And still another theory is that bands were invented to protect fingers and gloves against stains and to secure poorly rolled wrappers.

Cigar bands have been reproduced in gold for his-and-her wedding rings. And in 1850 Gustave Bock, a Havana cigar manufacturer who was concerned about cigar counterfeiters, made cigar bands with his own likeness on them. Soon heads of state from many parts of the world were ordering from him custom cigar bands bearing their likenesses or monograms. Edward VII and Winston Churchill of Great Britain, Prince Otto von Bismarck of Germany, and Franklin Delano Roosevelt had such personalized bands.

Wrapper Color Classifications

Claro claro—light green to greenish brown. Very mild and sometimes sweet or bitter. Very little oil. Also called candela or American market select.

Claro—light tan. Smooth smoking with neutral flavor. Usually shade grown. Traditionally the color of Connecticut shade wrapper.

Natural—light brown to brown. Fuller flavor than claro, but still smooth smoking. Usually sun grown.

Colorado claro—medium brown, tawny, slightly darker than claro. Smooth smoking with neutral flavor. Cameroon and Indonesian wrappers are this color.

Colorado—brown to reddish brown. Rich flavor and subtle aroma. A favorite color on well-matured cigars.

Colorado madura—dark brown. Rich flavored and aromatic. Grown from Havana seeds. Many Honduran cigars are this color.

Maduro—dark brown to very dark brown. Rich, strong flavor, slightly sweet; strong, unique aroma; slow burning. Leaves have matured longer in the sun. Have more texture, are oily looking. Not recommended for indoor smoking. A wrapper for seasoned smokers only.

Oscuro—very dark brown or almost black. Very strong with little bouquet. The wrapper of most Brazilian cigars. Clarissimo smokers consider them unsmokable.

To remove or not to remove, *that* is the question. The cigar band has created a controversial idiosyncrasy. The decision to remove the band or to leave it on is purely an aesthetic one. In the United States and on the European continent, it is a matter of choice. In Britain, however, it is considered "bad form" to advertise the brand that you are smoking—too ostentatious.

If you decide to remove the band, make sure that it isn't stuck to the wrapper leaf, or else it will make a hole in the wrapper. Slide the band carefully over the cigar's head. Never attempt to cut the band off—that almost guarantees damage to the wrapper. It's easier to slide the wrapper off after the cigar has been burning for some time. The heat in the cigar softens the glue and allows the band to slide off more easily. For the record, nearly 70 percent of cigar smokers remove the band. However, the band does have its practical uses: It can serve as a mark at which to stop smoking, and it indicates which end is which.

Man versus Machine

Like most other industries, the cigar industry has replaced people with machines and for the same reasons: Machines require less labor and are less expensive because they allow cigar makers to use "sheet" tobacco—tobacco and tobacco by-products that are pulverized into powder and pressed into sheets, similar to the way paper is made. More than 90 percent of all cigars manufactured in the United States include some sheet tobacco. It's used mostly as binder, but often as wrappers, too. Machines can make up to six hundred cigars per minute. A person can make only twenty-five an hour by hand.

There are three ways to make a cigar:

Handmade—The entire cigar is bunched, rolled, trimmed, and capped by hand.

Machine bunched/handrolled—The cigar's bunch is made by machine, then the wrapper is handrolled onto the cigar, and the cap is attached by hand.

Machine made—The cigar is made completely by machine.

Manufacturers may call their cigar assembly a number of things, but in reality their cigars are made in one of these three ways.

The consumer can be easily misled when a cigar is claimed to be handmade for the simple reason that U.S. law allows manufacturers to make such a claim even if a cigar is machine bunched or totally machine made with the exception of the cap, which is attached by hand. Anything done to a cigar by hand allows the maker to claim that it is handmade.

Machine-made cigars are looser and spongier than those that are handmade. They burn faster, too. Machine-made cigars are cheaper, and their ash does not get as long. Some cigars of 100 percent tobacco are machine made in part. Until 1935, all cigars were 100 percent tobacco.

But a machine-made cigar is not necessarily a bad cigar. Machinery can test the draw of a cigar and can allow cigars to be made more quickly, thus reducing the price to the smoker.

A handmade cigar, however, is the finest available. In the hands of a master craftsman, cigar making becomes an art form. Handmade cigars are highly prized (and highly priced) for their quality of construction and ingredients. They usually have a better draw, longer and whiter ash, and a more pleasing appearance.

A Grain of Sand

So what is a cigar? It is a complex creation involving dedication, patience, and skill—and love. Making a cigar is somewhat like raising a child: a work of art tinged with the complexities of confidence, power, and pleasure; a part of the personality of the one who smokes it. It's many things to many people. George Sand summed it up nicely: "The cigar numbs sorrow and fills the solitary hours with a million gracious images."

CHAPTER 4

SELECTION

Subjective Sophistication

As a woman of the nineties, you're called upon to make many high-level decisions. From the moment in the morning when you start orchestrating multifaceted events at home until you leave your similarly multifaceted workplace, there's no way to count how many times a day you've *decided* what course of action to follow. You certainly are well equipped to make your own decision about selecting a cigar.

No one can tell you how a cigar *should* taste or smell—that must be your own decision. As a rule, choosing a cigar is like choosing food and wine: If you like the taste and aroma, it's good. The subjectivity of taste is one of life's fascinations, and it definitely applies to cigars. Whatever pleases you is what you should smoke. But that doesn't mean that others can't help you in your search for the cigar, or cigars, that are just right for you.

The same cigar blend tastes different in different ring gauges and lengths. Ring gauge is the measure of the diameter of a cigar. Each unit of a ring gauge equals one sixty-fourth of an inch. Therefore, a cigar with a sixty-four ring gauge is one inch thick. The ring gauge of sixty-four is the largest there is. Ring gauge is the biggest influence of taste. A big ring gauge produces an immense volume of smoke. If you find one cigar that you like, that doesn't mean it will be as good in a different gauge.

Time of day does, however, help to determine what kind of cigar you may choose to smoke. Most people, particularly women, choose to smoke milder, smaller cigars in the morning or after a light lunch. A *robusto* is sometimes the choice after a heavy lunch—that's a lot of flavor packed into a reasonably short smoke. Bigger, more full-bodied cigars are usually saved for after dinner or for the evening. Most cigar smoking *is* done after dinner. Smoking before dinner plays havoc with your taste buds.

Pay attention to consistency—it's the key to good selection. In a box of cigars, the last one should taste as good as the first one, if not better. A good cigar is like fine wine—the aging process has an effect on the flavor, and, if a cigar or wine is aged properly, that effect will be positive.

It's preferable that all cigars in the same box have the same color. Usually, a box will contain twenty-five cigars. They should feel and look smooth when you roll them in your fingers. Generally, tobacco stores will allow you to purchase single cigars. Be sure to pick up a cigar by its foot rather than by its head. The cap could be damaged, or the head could be accidentally squeezed, ruining the draw of the cigar. This is a pet peeve of tobacconists. They do *not* want you to touch the head. Nor do you: That's the end that you put into your mouth!

Cigar QC: Quality

Obviously, quality control is as important in making cigars as it is in making any other product. The production of cigars requires constant oversight from "stalk to smoke." This process may extend up to three years.

Seven variables demand unremitting attention: blending of tobaccos, construction, quality and condition of wrappers, consistency, burning qualities, aromatic fragrances and bouquet, and taste and flavor.

If you are a novice cigar smoker, you will soon become adept at selecting cigars that have been given dedicated attention to details. Cigar aficionados know that you cannot tell what a cigar is going to be like as a smoke until it is smoked. Nevertheless, as you become more knowledgeable, your selections will reflect confidence and authority. Exercise your own quality control.

One source for cigar rating is the magazine *Cigar Aficionado*, which is published quarterly. Its staff experts frequently rate different cigars.

Cigar Size

Most women are in charge of purchasing clothing for their children, often for their husbands, and for themselves whether married or single. Size designations in different brands of clothing can vary greatly and be confusing. If you've ever shopped in a foreign country, you know that sizes are quite different than in the United States.

Well, if you haven't already, you'll soon learn that sizing systems are important for cigars, too. The ring gauge and shape designation of a cigar are called its *vitola* and impart very important information.

There is a direct relationship between the draw resistance of a cigar and its ring gauge. Large-ring cigars have less resistance than do small-ring cigars. Smokers want *some* resistance. On the other hand, the biggest complaint of cigar smokers is when the draw is too hard.

Experts have pontificated for years over the relationship between a person's physical appearance and cigar size. Cubans have a saying: "As you approach thirty, you have a thirty ring gauge; as you approach fifty, you have a fifty ring gauge."

Men tend to pair women with smaller cigars like Schimmelpennincks or with cigarillos. Smoking a fat cigar when you are small or thin *can* look rather comical or pretentious. For example, a *robusto* is a fat, short cigar—four inches long with a fifty-plus ring gauge. A Margarita is a very small cigar, as tiny as a cigarillo. However, the size of the cigar that you smoke is entirely up to you. Women are ready to move out of the cigarillo/demitasse niche.

The Eyes Have it: Appearance

Take a good look at a cigar. Its appearance can tell you a lot. A great cigar will have a smooth, flawless wrapper, consistency in color and shape, a slight "oily" feel, and be firm but not hard to the touch. Large veins, holes or other marks, and a rough finish are defects. However, small spots of a different color are nothing to worry about. Most likely they are water spots and have no effect on the cigar whatsoever.

Color Coded

It is the color of the filler, *not* the color of the wrapper, that reflects the strength of a cigar. The darker the tobacco, the more body and strength. The paler the tobacco, the milder and lighter it will smoke. A wrapper leaf alone cannot change the taste or strength of a cigar.

There are six major color grades for tobacco, rated by order of lightness:

1. *Claro claro* or *candela*—Light green leaves are cured with heat to fix chlorophyll in the leaf. Tends to taste slightly sweet or bitter. Not a popular color today.
2. *Claro*—light tan. Usually grown under shade tents. Prized for neutral flavor qualities.
3. *Colorado*—brown to reddish brown. Usually shade grown. Rich flavor and subtle aroma.
4. *Natural*—light brown to brown. Most often sun grown.
5. *Maduro*—dark brown. Ripened longer. Rich, strong flavor, mild aroma.
6. *Oscuro*—a swarthy cigar, almost black. Left on plant the longest.

Shape

There's a misconception that the larger the cigar, the stronger it will be. Actually, the fatter the cigar, the milder the taste. Shape is generally the driving force for cigar consumers today—away from middle-sized toward long and short: long when you have the time, short when you don't and would like a quick smoke.

All cigars can be divided into two shapes: *parejos* (straight sides) and *figurados* (irregular shapes). Cigars had standard shapes and sizes until factories started making their own unique cigars and giving them special names. Consequently, the old standard shapes are no more. A Churchill used to be eight and one-half inches long.

Today it's six and three-quarters to eight inches.

The following are names given to popular *figurado* cigars:

> Pyramid—pointed, closed head; widens to open foot
>
> *Belicoso*—small pyramid; head is round, not pointed
>
> Torpedo—both ends closed; bulge in middle— looks like cartoon cigar
>
> *Culebra*—three panatelas braided together
>
> *Diadema*—eight inches or longer; open foot most of the time

Smoke it Softly, Smoke it Slowly

A cool smoke is a tastier smoke because coolness means that the tobacco isn't carbonizing or overheating, which can limit the flavor. Draw and burn are the most important factors affected by construction.

A large-ring cigar has a better blend ratio than does a small-ring cigar. A long cigar will smoke cooler and milder than will a short cigar for the obvious reason that the tuck is farther away. Cigars of nine and a half inches can take up to two hours to smoke. The girth of a small-ring cigar makes it harder to blend enough different tobaccos to give the cigar complexity and strength. Such a cigar is best suited for smokers who are not looking for big taste. Compare the smoking time of about an hour for a Lonsdale to the smoking time of about three hours for a Montecristo "A." Generally speaking, the shorter the cigar, the shorter the time for smoking pleasure.

If all this seems like a lot of information to absorb, you're right! You can use this book as a guide. The following should help you to make your selections:

Cigarillo—a seven- to ten-minute smoke. Though popular in Europe, cigarillos have never caught on in the United States. Always machine made. When cigar smoking is not allowed, but cigarette smoking is, you might get lucky if you pull out one of these. Many times cigarillos will pass as cigarettes.

Robusto—thick ring gauge and short length. *Robustos* are popular because they can be smoked in a relatively short period of time—thirty to forty-five minutes—after lunch or before dinner. Great flavor in an easy-smoking size. Can be smoked without losing any ash.

Panatela—long and thin and known for a mild flavor. For years it has been the choice of the tall, thin smoker—reflecting the cigar/body type legend. It provides forty to forty-five minutes of smoking pleasure. Length, five inches; ring gauge, twenty-six.

Petit corona—small category. Short length and relatively thin. Ring gauge, thirty-eight to forty-four; length, five to five and a half inches. This size is not a brand's benchmark size. Offers a modest amount of smoking pleasure in a short period of time—about forty minutes. Prices are lower than those of a corona because of less tobacco. Good things come in small packages.

Corona—Spanish for "crown." This is the king of cigars because of its ideal size and tobacco blending. The archetypal handrolled cigar, it is the standard for measuring quality. Easy to handle and of intermediate length and ring gauge. One of average size provides forty-five to sixty minutes of smoking pleasure: three-fourths of the cigar will have been consumed—almost to the band.

Lonsdale—named for the earl of Lonsdale. Ring gauge of forty-two to forty-three, six to six and three-quarters inches long. The Montecristo #1 is considered the definitive Lonsdale. Its smoke time is fifty to sixty minutes.

Double corona—considered the Rolls-Royce of cigars. Its thick girth and long length allow makers better opportunity to blend and balance tobacco. It is a full-flavored smoke. More than an hour of smoking pleasure.

Churchill—named after Winston Churchill, it was his favorite. It has the size that befits a great statesman.

It's a big, full-bodied cigar—seven inches long, forty-seven ring gauge. Smoking time of an hour or more.

Whether robust or subtle, a great cigar should taste smooth, rich, and full. There should be no bitterness or harshness on the lips, tongue, or in the mouth while smoking. Aftertaste should be smooth and clean. There even are cigars with flavors such as spicy, cocoa, and coffee. You might want to try them!

Brands and Bands: Manufacturers

You'll find the brand name of a cigar on the band. However, depending on the country you're in, the same name can come from two different companies. Some brands, such as Romeo y Julieta, Punch, Partagas, Macanudo, and Davidoff, were first produced in Cuba. During Castro's revolution in 1960, many manufacturers fled and believed that they could take their brand names with them. The Cubans argued that the names belonged to the country, so today you see the same names but different origins. However, a small "Habana" inscribed on the band will mean that the cigar is Cuban made.

Cuban cigars have long been considered to be the best in the world. However, this is changing. Because demand is up, Cubatabaco—the government tobacco monopoly—has been cutting corners on fermentation and is using tobacco that may not be up to the old standards. The top-quality tobacco is just not as available as it used to be.

Also, Cubans do not replace their wooden bunch molds every four years like manufacturers in most other countries do. The edges of bunch molds break down over time, and the shape of the cigars becomes less consistent. Cubans also don't use the latest technology to guarantee consistent draw and do not use tobacco from other parts of the world that may have had a better growing year.

Because of these circumstances, other countries,

such as the Dominican Republic (the refuge of many Cuban cigar makers who fled from Castro), are overtaking Cuba's cigar industry.

Lighting the Way: The Tobacconist

Most cigar lovers depend on their tobacconist to supply their favorite smokes. You should buy only from tobacconists who have a well-run humidor. Glass-counter displays can be a bad sign because regulating the climate in them is difficult. Be sure to inspect the cigars and check that there is a temperature and humidity gauge in the area where they are kept.

Be careful in your selection of a tobacconist. And then trust him or her, not other smokers, for advice. However, you must tell your tobacconist what you want in a cigar—mild, premium, etc.

The process of cigar selection begins at the tobacconist's. There are so many kinds of cigars on the market that, to find your preference, you simply must sample a few. Your tobacconist can help you with your initial selections.

Fools Rush In

Sometimes a cigar manufacturer will have a roller from the factory at a smoke shop or at a smoker (cigar-smoking event), rolling cigars and giving them away to observers. This is an interesting and effective marketing concept. However, a cigar should not be smoked immediately after rolling because the moisture content in the binder and wrapper is too high. For the roller, the moisture needs to be high so that the tobacco is pliable and rolls on easily, but for the smoker, the cigar should be allowed to cure in a humidor for two weeks before smoking.

"Have the box opened first" is a basic bit of advice for buying any cigar. That way you can see general packing and first-row quality. If you are not allowed to touch a cigar, be suspicious. However, you'll find 99 percent of the tobacconists to be friendly and eager to help you. They'll take all the time necessary to guide you in your selections. As in any good—and competitive—business, the tobacconist's main concern is to earn your trust and respect.

Boxes of twenty-five with two layers always have thirteen on the first row. The designation "8-9-8" is a three-layer box of twenty-five: eight in the first and last layers, nine in the middle layer. Opening the box allows you to assess color and quality of the wrapper. Visiting a tobacco shop and its humidifier is the best way to become familiar with the different shapes and sizes of cigars.

When inspecting cigars before buying, if you notice that the tuck (foot) of a cigar has frayed edges, this does not mean that the cigar is too dry. It means that the knife used in the factory to cut the end was dull.

Continuity is crucial to a good tobacco shop—in few other businesses do the employees stay on as long as they do in tobacco shops. Indeed, you won't find minimum-wage workers here. Most are true aficionados and are extremely knowledgeable about their inventory. Eventually you will get to know the people who help you in the shops that you frequent most often.

Heavy traffic at a tobacco shop is a good sign that supplies are fresh because of high turnover. The tobacconist should entertain your requests for special orders and should not try to sell you his store brands. He should be current on market changes and should know what kind of tobaccos are being used.

An alternative way to buy is in "bundle cigars." This practice started in the 1960s as a way to buy cigars more cheaply because you don't pay manufacturer's cost of color sorting and cedar boxes. The cigars in bundles tend not to have consistent wrapper color; however, this is a perfectly acceptable way to buy cigars.

Dollars and Sense: Price

Know what you are paying for. Cigar pricing is influenced by the quality of tobacco used, taxation, packaging, labor, and importation costs. Also by the manufacturing process. The handmade process requires extra effort and time, which results in higher prices. Less expensive cigars may have additives such as saltpeter, propylene glycol, and glycerin to enhance flavor and prevent drying.

Prices vary a great deal. At the upper end of the scale, cigars go for eighty to three hundred dollars per box. Fancy packaging can add greatly to the overall cost. Individual aluminum or glass tubes and elaborate canisters cost money without contributing much to taste. Polished and beveled cedar or mahogany boxes or gift selections of five to ten cigars increase the cost as well.

Men tend to be swayed by label and price when buying a good cigar. They feel that these determine whether a cigar is good.

Women, on the other hand, historically are not influenced by label and price. They look for a price-to-quality ratio. Maybe this is because they generally do more shopping or because they have been exposed to more phony marketing programs. Currently, cigar pricing has little correlation with actual quality. Manufacturers will introduce a cigar at a higher price to build image, whereas another cigar that they make for less could actually be of better quality. The biggest determinant in cost of a fine cigar

is the tobacco. However, some states heavily tax cigars. For example, Washington state has such a high tax that there are few smoke shops, and most Washington cigar smokers shop by mail order.

Tobacco stores are still the best source unless you know exactly what you want, but buying cigars from mail-order companies is becoming more popular because such companies let you buy at discounted prices and avoid state taxes. However, mail-order purchasing requires that you buy in volume. You cannot buy singles. Always have the cigars shipped overnight or second-day delivery to reduce their chances of being dried out in transit.

And, lastly, don't judge a cigar by its box—some inferior cigars have the most elaborate packaging.

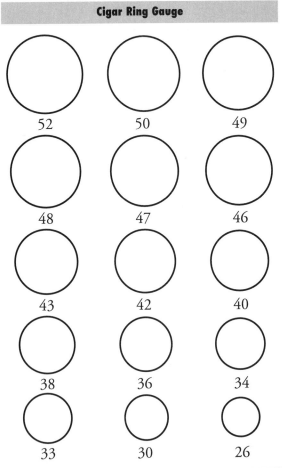

Cigar Ring Gauge

52 50 49

48 47 46

43 42 40

38 36 34

33 30 26

The numbers represent the diameter of holes in 64ths of an inch.

CHAPTER 5

QUOTABLES

They Said a Mouthful

It seems that everyone of any renown who smokes cigars wants to express his or her sentiments about them. Such smokers haven't always been eloquent, but their ideas illuminate their personalities and are often humorous and entertaining—to those who don't smoke cigars as well as to those who do. So, just for the fun of it, light up that great cigar that's been waiting to join you in some special moment of relaxation and pleasure. And be entertained.

> "There's peace in a Larranaga, there's calm in a Henry Clay,
> And a woman is only a woman, but a good cigar is a smoke."
>
> *Rudyard Kipling*

> "A woman is just a script, but a cigar is a motion picture."
>
> *Samuel Fuller*
> movie director
> parody of Kipling

"After a truly good meal, an outstanding cigar is still the most satisfying
after-dinner activity that doesn't
involve two human beings."

Brad Shaw
Radio announcer

A cigar has "...a fire at one end and a
fool at the other."

Horace Greeley
founder of the *New York Tribune*

"Women   are   really   jealous   of
cigars...they regard them as a strong
rival."

William Makepeace Thackeray
English author

"If a woman knows a man's preferences,
including his preference in cigars,
and if a man knows what a woman
likes, they will be suitably armed to
face one another."

Colette
French author
in *Gigi*

"My boy! Smoking is one of the greatest
and cheapest enjoyments in life, and
if you decide in advance not to
smoke, I can only feel sorry for you."

Sigmund Freud
comment to seventeen-year-old nephew
Harry after he declined a cigar

"If I paid $10 for a cigar, first I'd make
love to it, then I'd smoke it."

George Burns

"Cigar smoking knows no politics. It's about the pursuit of pleasure, taste, and aroma."

Anonymous

"Every cigar goes up in smoke."

Brazilian proverb

"If the birth of a genius resembles that of an idiot, the end of a Havana Corona resembles that of a 5-cent cigar."

Sasha Guitry
French actor

"If you kiss a cigar—it will kiss you back. If you treat it like a dog—it will turn around and bite you."

George Brightman
Cigar Aficionado magazine

"Smoking is indispensable if one has nothing to kiss."

Sigmund Freud
in letter to future wife Martha Bernays
during a long absence

"Do not ask me to describe the charms of reverie, or the contemplative ecstasy into which the smoke of our cigar plunges us."

Jules Sandea
French novelist

"A good cigar is as great a comfort to a man as a good cry to a woman."

E. G. Bulwer-Lytton
Darnley, 1845

"A good cigar is like tasting a good
  wine: you smell it, you taste it, you
  look at it, You feel it—you can even
  hear it. It satisfies all the senses."
                                    Anonymous

"Earth ne'er did breed
  Such a jovial weed."
                            Barten Holyday
                         Technogamia, 1618

"He who has money smokes cigars
  But who has no money smokes paper."
                         an old Spanish saying

"What this country needs is a good
  5-cent cigar."
                            Thomas Marshall
                   Woodrow Wilson's vice president
                      stated in the Senate in 1919

"Eating and sleeping are the only activities that should be allowed to inter-
  rupt a man's enjoyment of his cigar."
                                 Mark Twain

"Where there's a good smoke there's a
  cigar smoker."
                                Cuban saying

"You kissed my trembling hand
  and on my finger you slipped
  An eighteen-carat cigar band."
  from the song "You'll be Reminded of Me"
              in the movie *Vivacious Lady*

"Cigars after dinner are delightful,
  Smoking before breakfast is unnatural."
                               Bernard Shaw

"Remember, commander, no cigars before launch."

Cuban doctor's orders to an astronaut at Cape Canaveral

"I do not seek for fame
    A general with a scar;
    A private let me be,
    So I have my cigar…
    Some sigh for this or that,
    My wishes don't go far;
    The world may wag at will,
    So I have my cigar."

Thomas Hood
English poet

"Darling, you must choose between me and your cigars."

Rudyard Kipling
The Betrothed, 1899

"Lady Bracknell: Do you smoke?
    Earnest: Well, yes, I must admit I smoke.
    Lady Bracknell: I am glad to hear it. A man should always have an occupation of some kind."

Oscar Wilde
The Importance of Being Earnest

"Lastly (and this is, perhaps, the golden rule), no woman should marry a man who does not smoke."

Robert Louis Stevenson
Virginibus Puerisque, 1881

"Light me another Cuban."

Rudyard Kipling
Departmental Ditties

"If your wife doesn't like the aroma of
your cigar—change your wife."

Zino Davidoff
cigar company founder

"Here, have a cigar. Light it up and be
somebody."

from the film Pete Kelly's Blues

"In the future all men will be able to
smoke Havanas."

Herr Doktor Schutte
an early Marxist

"'Now look,' she said, 'either dance
with me—or the cigar.'
Sammy jerked the cigar from his
mouth as if it were a stopper check-
ing his flow of words."

Budd Schulberg
What Makes Sammy Run

"To smoke is human; to smoke cigars is
divine."

Unknown

"By the cigars they smoke, and the
composers they love,
ye shall know the texture of men's
souls."

John Galsworthy

"Gentlemen, you may smoke."

King Edward VII
words spoken after his inaugural dinner,
sending England the message that cigar
smoking was once again acceptable

"If I cannot smoke in heaven, then I shall not go."

Mark Twain

"I am sure there are many things better than a good cigar, but right now, I can't think of what they might be."

Richard Carleton
cigar authority and author

"Now here's Bud Scott
And his old guitar,
Always smoking his big cigar."

Louis Armstrong
introduction of one of his jazz pals

"Cognac and cigars...it's like finding the perfect woman. When you've got her, why go chasing after another?"

Michael Nouri
actor

"Cigar smoking actively encouraged."

sign in a London restaurant

"There was a young man of Herne Bay
who was making some fireworks one
        day:
but he dropped his cigar
in the gunpowder jar.
There *was* a young man of Herne Bay."

Ogden Nash

"The two Christians met on the way many people who were going to their towns, women and men, with a fire-brand in the hand, and certain weeds whose smoke they inhale which are dry weeds stuffed into a certain dry leaf in the form of a muset made of paper, like the ones the children make the day of the Holy Ghost; and burning a part of it, from the other part they suck or absorb or admit the smoke with breathing."

Christopher Columbus
navigation diary

"The best cigar in the world is the one you prefer to smoke on special occasions, enabling you to relax and enjoy that which gives you maximum pleasure."

Zino Davidoff

Size and Shape

Popular Sizes and Their Measurements

Size	Length in Inches	Ring Gauge
Demitasse	4	30
Panatela	4.5	26
Petit corona	5	42
Robusto	5	50
Corona	5.5	42
Belicoso	5.5	52
Culebra (3)	5.75	39
Lonsdale	6.5	42
Pyramid/torpedo	6.25	52
Churchill	7	47
Double corona	7.75	49

"Given the choice between a woman and a cigar, I will always choose the cigar."

Groucho Marx

"A good Cuban cigar closes the door to the vulgarities of the world."

Franz Liszt
composer

"The most futile and disastrous day seems well spent when it is reviewed through the blue, fragrant smoke of a Havana cigar."

Evelyn Waugh
English writer

"There are two things a man never forgets—his first love and his first cigar."

John Bain
Cigar lover

"That's close, but no cigar."

Well-known saying of carnival barkers

CHAPTER 6

HOW TO SMOKE A CIGAR

The Why and the Why Not

Personal style is the quality that attracts us most to others. It is our personal blueprint for how we do things as individuals. Cigar smoking has its own style, too. Since its creation, the cigar has bestowed respect and stature upon the smoker; it has been a *bon vivant's* scepter of cultivated taste and pleasure. How a cigar is handled says a great deal about a person and his or her style.

Women, like men, find many reasons to smoke cigars. Smoking enhances a sense of joy when we are celebrating the birth of a child, a wedding, a promotion, or just completing a fine meal. It's part of the good life, like a fine bottle of wine or champagne.

Winston Churchill had his own style. He was known to dunk the head of his cigar into a glass of fine wine. Although many cigar lovers feel that this practice shows a lack of respect for the time and skill that went into making the cigar and ruins its flavor, it was Churchill's style and choice. The truth about this practice is that it is best to sip your wine or spirits between draws. This way you enjoy both to the fullest.

Each cigar has its own smell and flavor—flavors like coffee, nuts, or chocolate. A cigar's flavor develops as you smoke it. Often its true potential is not revealed until the halfway point when the tobacco has been warmed and the flavors are blending. If you choose to smoke more than one cigar a day, subsequent cigars should have equal or fuller flavor. If you smoke a full-flavored cigar and then one with a lighter flavor, you will not taste the latter.

Some women have been known to smoke cigars for their rich tobacco buzz or for the way that cigars bring back the art of conversation. Other women smoke for nostalgia—Dad or Uncle smoked, and they learned to like the aroma. Still others use cigar smoking as a prop.

Unlike men, very few women smoke cigars to show that they have climbed the ladder of success. They smoke cigars mostly for social reasons. For instance, if a woman offered a man a cigar on a date, the two of them would sit down together and talk. Likewise when two women get together. This is a good example of how cigars help to develop the art of conversation. Cigars, because of their length, require a chunk of time to be enjoyed fully. A date with one's husband, boyfriend, or a woman friend could be arranged simply by asking, "Do you want to go out for a cigar?" rather than for a drink or dinner or a movie.

Don't Smoke the Smoke if…

A Latin proverb, "*stylus virum arguit*," cautioned that "our style betrays us," and it's true. In more recognizable vernacular, "actions speak louder than words." Don't talk the talk if you can't walk the walk! Cigar-smoking women *are* confident. They like to have fun, but, more than likely, image making is not a priority for them. If you wish to develop a cigar-smoking style that says who you are, there are some guidelines that most women follow.

You should let a man light your cigar for you, in the same way that you let him prepare a drink for you. If the man is your husband or special friend, perhaps he gives a little instruction, especially if he is a smoker. If a man lights a cigar for you, he should not put it into his mouth. The way a man prepares the cigar and lights it will tell you a lot about him. Don't consider it a condescending act. Rather, accept it as a kind gesture and watch and learn. However, lighting technique is a very individual art. If you feel strongly about a certain way of lighting, you should not be chastised for doing it yourself. But don't make the man feel like he's dealing with a defiant woman.

No discriminating cigar smoker, under any circumstances, inhales the smoke. It can cause vertigo, a headache, and a hangover. The true joy of smoking a cigar comes from allowing the taste buds to savor the extraordinary combination of flavors of the smoke.

As you smoke a cigar, swirl the smoke around your mouth and then blow it out (this technique also avoids the addiction problem associated with cigarette smoking). As a person exhales, half of the smoke can be blown through the nose. Many cigar smokers find this pleasurable. The sensation has been described as smoke washing over your brain. However, this technique is not recommended for women because it doesn't look attractive.

To paraphrase an observation attributed to Homer and Palladas, "Many things happen between the cigar and the lip."

A Cut Above: Cutting

One of the most extraordinary rituals in the world of connoisseurship is the cutting of a cigar. But if it's done incorrectly, or with a dull blade, there will be unfortunate results:

- Smoke will be hot.
- Damaged wrapper leaf will unravel.
- Draw will be difficult.—Unsightly bits of tobacco will be left in your mouth and teeth. Removal of them is awkward, not to mention inelegant.

- ☞ Tobacco will be damaged.
- ☞ Cigar will be ruined.

The cut should be absolutely clean. Therefore, it is important that the cutter be sharp. You should leave about one-eighth of an inch of the cap. Never cut a cigar on or below cap level. The cap helps keep the wrapper leaf from unraveling. The goal is to clip off enough of the end to expose the filler leaves, but to leave enough of the cap or flap to keep the wrapper on the cigar. It is also preferable that the edge of the head have a slight rounding. This is particularly advantageous to women because it helps minimize lipstick marks on the cigar and leaves lipstick where it should be—on the lips.

The cut must be large enough for the cigar to draw properly—slightly smaller than the diameter of the body of the cigar and perpendicular to the edges. A common mistake is not making the cut wide enough.

One cutting method to be avoided is piercing a small hole in the center of the head of the cigar. Piercing is not recommended because it compresses the tobacco into a lump, which impedes the draw. Also, the smoke drawn is concentrated through a little hole. Because the cigar will not draw well, there's a greater chance of getting tar and resins into the mouth. The "tunnel" inside created by piercing will act like a sump, collecting tar from the filler and channeling it straight onto your tongue.

The size of the hole made by the cut is very important. If the hole is too large, it permits too great a rush of smoke into the mouth. The smoke volume will be difficult to regulate, and your cigar will smoke faster. The filler in short-filler cigars will end up in your mouth. The wrapper and part of the binder will begin to unravel, loosening the cigar and looking unsightly. The cigar will be such a nuisance to smoke that you will be better off to throw it away and start with a new one.

On the other hand, if the hole is too small, smoke is forced through a restricted opening. This increases resistance and causes you to have to draw more for less smoke. You now have a chore rather than a pleasure in your hands. You will also find the bitter taste of nicotine on your lips and in your mouth because the suction necessary to draw will concentrate the tar and other oils to the hole. This blankets the flavor and burns the tongue.

A Slice of Life: Cutting Options

Simple tools have been designed to remove the capped head of your cigar before smoking. These include the guillotine, the wedge cut, the bull's eye, and piercers; each performs the cutting action in a distinctly different way. The flat cutters slice the end off of the head. The V-shaped cutters cut a slice out, across the head, and leave a deceptively large surface area. Do not cut too deep. Not surprisingly, Churchill used the V-shaped cut during World War II.

Swiss scissors can take a chunk off of the cigar, plungers take a neat plug out of the cigar, and there also are piercing drills.

If you're going to smoke the cigar shortly after purchasing it, a good suggestion is to allow the tobacconist to cut the head off for you. This will guarantee that it is done correctly, eliminate the need for you to have a cutter, and let you avoid handling the scraps of tobacco left after the cut.

Closed-head cigars must be cut before the tuck (foot) is lighted. This can be done with one of the tools mentioned earlier, a knife, or your teeth. The latter, however, is acceptable only in a crunch. Using your teeth is very risky. Only skilled experts who smoke a lot can do this correctly. You can't see the cut while you're making it and thus risk tearing the flap or cap. And spitting out what you bite off is unsightly.

Nor should you emulate Princess Margaret of Great Britain, who was alleged to have used her lacquered fingernails to cut the head off of her cigars—royalty is not *always* correct.

Women should use only a cigar cutter. If you must use a knife, be sure to rotate the cigar on the blade in the same direction as the wrapper was wound onto the binder.

Hand to Mouth: Smoking

Smoking style is something that you come by on your own. There are some things, however, that you may want to consider. It's important that you master the beauty of your hands and lips. Enjoy the way the cigar sits in your hand. Roll it between your fingers—get acquainted with it. You will find that different ring gauges feel better than others. Hold the cigar in a way that feels natural. You can hold it between two or three fingers, but before lighting up, hold it between your thumb and index finger and *gently* squeeze. The cigar should feel slightly springy. The wrapper should feel like silk, and a sheen from the natural oils might be present as well.

While it's being smoked, a cigar should be held between its middle and head and *not* squeezed. Squeezing can block the smoke's passage through the body of the cigar and can cause it to go out.

There are many ways to hold a cigar; for example, held between two fingers, held between three fingers with the index finger curled over the top, or held from underneath. There is no single right way. However, it should look natural and effortless.

The cigar should never leave your hand except when you place it in an ashtray. The cigar should be held away from your face, your clothing, and your hair. This disseminates the smoke and odor more evenly and limits the amount that infiltrates your hair and garments. The cigar should be kept away from other people for the same reason; moving your cigar from one hand to the other is one way of showing this consideration of others.

A woman should shape her lips in the form of a kiss so that they encircle the cigar. The inner lips should touch the outside of the cigar, with the teeth touching—not biting—the cigar to stabilize it. This keeps your lipstick off of the cigar—something that you especially want to pay attention to if you're sharing a cigar with a man.

Chewing on the head of a cigar is not recommended—it is simply bad form and the sign of an amateur (chewing tobacco and snuff *are* available). Chewing damages the cigar, making it almost impossible to smoke. The cigar head should have a good mouth feel—firm and resilient. If it is soft and mushy, that's another sign of poor construction.

While holding a lighted cigar, keep the tip up. This ensures that the ash stays on longer, that you can keep an eye on it, and that your nails and hands won't smell of smoke. Besides, it looks more elegant.

The draw of a cigar smoker should be smooth and steady. The smoke should be cool in your mouth. The ash should burn white and even and hold for at least one inch before falling.

It is best to smoke a cigar after a good meal. A full stomach eliminates any bad effects from the absorption of nicotine through your mouth and gums. Avoid smoking on an empty stomach. Even if you're not inhaling, it could cause nausea.

Smoke a cigar until it no longer tastes good. This *can* occur when only half of the cigar has been smoked. When approximately two-thirds or three-fourths has been smoked, or when you are nearing the band, stop smoking. It's bad form to smoke to the band or to let it catch on fire. Leave the cigar in an ashtray to go out on its own. Do not stub it out. The butt has harsh flavor and holds most of the tar from the entire cigar. The tar will soon extinguish the fire.

It is not unusual to experience increased salivation when you smoke a cigar for the first time. This is another reason to smoke with a full stomach. The food tends to draw saliva to the stomach.

As you create your own style, an image will emerge—an image of a competent, confident, adventurous, and, yes, fun-loving woman.

The Light Fantastic: Lighting

The act of lighting a cigar is very intimate and personal. Never rush it. It is part of the ritual and enjoyment of a good cigar. You can recognize an aficionado as one who pays close attention to the lighting process. When a gentleman offers to light your cigar, the act can be a romantic overture, like the sharing of food. Carefully consider the message sent by a refusal or an acceptance. A woman's request that a man light her cigar can also be a romantic overture. If a man lights a cigar for you, it should be "toasted" while in his hand, not lit while in his mouth. He should hand it to you lighted.

Don't hold a cigar in your mouth while lighting it. Men can and do, but women should not. You'll look unattractively like a blowfish. Instead, take your time, use more matches—or a lighter—and look ladylike. Don't sacrifice your femininity for speed.

"Toasting" is the best way for a woman to light her cigar. Hold it in your hand at a forty-five-degree angle over the flame. Light the open tuck end, making sure not to let the flame touch the cigar. Touching the flame to the cigar makes it too black. And when you plunge a cigar into the heart of a flame, you turn the tobacco into carbon, and the smoke tastes hot and harsh. As you smoke, the cigar will continue to taste cooked because you'll be sucking air across a burnt surface. Keep the flame about one-fourth inch from the tuck and rotate the cigar slowly so that the toasting is even. Eventually, a blue flame will jump up and rise from the top of the tuck. The rim of the tuck should begin to glow first, then the fire will begin to spread to the center.

Now gently blow on the tuck to ensure that your cigar is burning evenly. If it is not, continue lighting in the places where the ember is missing. Check one more time with a light blow, then place the cigar in your mouth and gently blow out first to remove any smoke that may have a flavor from the match or lighter. Now sit back and enjoy your cigar. Note: The larger the cigar's ring gauge, the more time and care needed to light it. Don't warm the length of the cigar before lighting it. This used to be done to burn off the unpleasant gum on Seville cigars. It isn't necessary today.

When one side of a cigar burns faster than the other but your lighting was even, it's called "tunneling." The cigar will never smoke right and will be a frustrating experience. When this happens, give it up and put it out. You'll be happier in the long run.

Rekindling the Flame: Relighting

A cigar cannot be ignored when being smoked. It will go out. Drawing on it regularly (about once a minute) will certainly keep it alive unless it is badly made or its humidity level is too high. However, should a cigar go out when you are enjoying it enough to want to continue, by all means relight it.

Before relighting, blow through the cigar to eliminate any lingering smoke that could cause the cigar to taste bitter. Next, remove all of the ash. This is commonly done with the nonstriking end of a match. The ash will have a cone shape inside your cigar, with the deepest point being in the middle. Now you are ready to relight. Apply the flame around the rim while turning the cigar. As long as the cigar does not carry too much ash, it will rekindle itself.

After relighting, the cigar will have a stronger flavor and some bitterness initially. A cigar not relighted within an hour of going out will never taste the same.

Preparing a cigar to be relighted can be a messy and awkward experience. If you are smoking in private and want to take on the task, go right ahead. However, if you are smoking in public, it might be best to call it quits.

Ashes to Ashes: Ash

The cigar ash has long been examined and revered, both for its color and for its staying power on the end of a cigar.

Some experts believe that the quality of a cigar can be determined merely by looking at its ashes: The paler the ashes, the better the cigar. A mediocre cigar has dark ashes, a bad one has black. Cigars command more respect when they produce a firm off-white or blue-gray ash. The truth about ash color is that it corresponds to the type of soil that the tobacco was grown in. The higher the magnesium content, the whiter the ash. A darker gray ash means that the cigar has a more robust flavor. Some cigar manufacturers have become clever and treat their lower-quality cigars with magnesium to create a whiter ash.

Less-than-premium cigars will have a flaky, soft ash of brown or black. If quality binder tobacco was used, the ash should be firm and able to burn to at least an inch long (except in small ring gauges) before it begins to disintegrate under its own weight. But a falling ash does not necessarily indicate a poorly constructed cigar. Wind or quick movements by the smoker can cause ash to fall prematurely. However, a consistently flaky, loose ash *is* a sign of poor construction. Splits in an ash indicate poor or loose filler.

Let the ash of a cigar reach at least three-quarters of an inch before flicking it, although it is actually better never to flick cigar ash like cigarette ash. The ash protects the ember and helps to keep the smoke temperature cool. Let the ash alone—allow it to fall off naturally into an ashtray. Sometimes it is advisable to take precautionary steps to remove the ash before it falls onto your clothing. To help the ash along, take two quick puffs before tipping your ash, then tap away neatly, exposing the cone-shaped ember. Allow the cigar to cool down for a few seconds after tipping the ash because the cigar is burning hot with an exposed ember and will *taste* hot. Ash buildup helps to keep the cigar lit. It is also believed that flicking an ash off before it is ready promotes uneven burning.

Another reason not to flick your ash is that doing so indicates that you are a novice. And a long ash shows other cigar smokers how well your cigar is made.

Fresh cigar ash could burn when it falls, although some smokers make a ritual out of tipping the ash into their hand and letting it cool before placing it into an ashtray. Don't let the ash accumulate *too* much unless you are paying close attention. Some ash should always be left on the cigar so that the smoke receives the full bouquet of the tobacco.

Cigar ash is quite different from cigarette ash. It is pure tobacco, not tobacco mixed with paper and other substances. Consequently, it is much easier to clean up. Cigar ash quickly breaks down into almost a powder, which is easily vacuumed up or brushed off. It leaves no stains or marks, unlike the carbon in cigarette ash.

There's a definite correlation between the construction of a cigar and the process of learning how to prepare it for a smoke that delivers the ultimate enjoyment.

CHAPTER 7

ETIQUETTE

What Would Emily Post Say?

Etiquette is the natural partner of style, and the two go together like "please" and "thank you." Mark Twain said, "Cigar smokers, as a general rule, are very polite people."

And, indeed, cigar smokers do consider themselves to be gentlemen and ladies. They pride themselves on showing courtesy before lighting up, on obeying local ordinances, and on disposing of their cigars properly.

Guidelines of etiquette apply to cigar smoking just as they should to all human interaction. The following are considerations that we should remember.

- Always ask, "May I?" of people around you before lighting a cigar.
- Locate an ashtray before lighting your cigar.
- Watch those ashes. When they fall, they are hot and can burn.
- If you are a demonstrative conversationalist, put down your cigar before talking with your hands.
- If you offer someone a cigar, never just hand it— offer it from an open humidor, box, or other container, allowing the recipient to select.
- Don't talk with your cigar in your mouth.

- ☞ Light up only after desert, not between courses.
- ☞ Do not kill a cigar as if it were a cigarette. Don't crush it by rubbing it against the ashtray. Simply leave it in the ashtray to die a natural death.
- ☞ Don't exit an establishment, such as a restaurant, with a cigar in your hand. The sidewalk and street are *not* places to discard your cigar stub.
- ☞ Cigar smoking should be sipping, not swigging. Take leisurely puffs.
- ☞ Hold smoke for five seconds, then exhale slowly. It's generally accepted that the cigar should be puffed one or two times a minute, which is enough to keep it lit but not so much that it becomes hot or harsh.
- ☞ Do not rush a cigar. Frantic puffing causes the cigar to burn with more heat and to taste hot. Frantic puffing also hurts the aroma.
- ☞ Do not smoke a cigar by retaining it in your mouth during most of the smoke. Hold it in your hand between puffs.
- ☞ Nineteenth-century women held their cigar delicately in a gloved hand. There aren't many occasions now when you wear gloves, but it is still proper to hold your cigar delicately and with your fingers always straight. However, a properly rolled and smoked cigar does not stain your fingers. It really isn't necessary any more to hold the cigar around the band.

Put Your Cigar Out...Please

As your woman's perspective of cigar etiquette develops, you are unlikely to commit the *faux pas* of offending anyone with your smoking. But even though you are courteous and considerate of other people, as are your lady and gentleman cigar-smoking peers, you may, on occasion, have to defend your rights.

Not many nonsmokers, especially those who dislike cigar smoke, would frequent places where cigars are smoked. However, when you are asked to put out your cigar, you should always take the high road and oblige or move.

A small book entitled *101 Ways to Answer the Request, Would You Please Put Out That #!&*!\$ Cigar* is a fun read. Although I do not recommend that any of its responses be used, some of the funnier ones are listed for your amusement:

- "Is it the smoke that bothers you, or the sight of someone enjoying himself?"
- "I'd love to, but I'm afraid you'd think I'm easy."
- "My parole officer says it steadies my nerves."
- "We are both blowing smoke, but I at least have the courtesy to be smoking a fine cigar."
- "Wait! Don't tell me! 'Put out that #\$%*&! cigar!' Bogey, *Casablanca*, 1943. And Ingrid Bergman replies, 'Why do I only get that from guys who are lousy in bed?'"
- "I've often wondered which is ruder: smoking a cigar or interrupting a total stranger."
- "No, but I'll defend to the death your right to ask me."
- "What a great icebreaker! I applaud your moxie. If I were of your class, I would never dream of approaching someone like me."
- "I'm an artist. My medium is smoke."
- "Doctors say people with sensitive noses are sexually repressed. Kiss me."
- "Does the smoke bother your nose job?"
- "Goodness, I admire people who aren't afraid to be disliked."
- "Don't you know I only have a week to live? Who put you up to this?"
- "Oops, I don't have an ashtray. Would you please pass me your plate?"
- "Why? Are you waiting for the butt?"
- "Sure, if you'll turn down the volume on your jacket."
- "How ironic…I lit this to keep you away."

Etiquette Elegance

It's true that cigar smoking is no longer a gender-specific practice, but you still want to maintain your femininity as well as your freedom of choice. Some traditional cigar practices frankly look more unsightly when done by a woman than by a man.

With that in mind, let's discuss how a cigar should work with a woman's mouth. When you place a cigar into your mouth, don't let your lips do all the work—the cigar can be heavy, and holding it too tightly between your lips will give you a strange facial expression. The head of the cigar will become wet as well. Put the cigar into your mouth (which is opened slightly larger than the cigar's girth) far enough that your teeth will hold it in place. Now put your lips lightly around the cigar, with only the inner lips touching it.

Avoid letting your cigar go out frequently. Relighting affects taste and aroma and can be distracting to your smoking companions.

Evening, especially after dinner, is considered the time of the cigar. Smoking a good cigar is the compliment—or complement—of a good meal. The heavier the meal you eat, the stronger the cigar should be. As a hostess you might want to suggest a cigar instead of dessert—cigars *are* fat- and cholesterol-free! In lieu of that, after dessert a fine cigar with an equally fine brandy is a wonderful way to complete the dining experience.

Entertaining: Extending and Accepting an Offer

If you choose to allow cigar smoking at a party that you are hosting, it is proper etiquette to bring out a humidor or box of cigars to offer to guests. If the event is a dinner party, the offer should be extended after dessert, with an alternate location offered if a guest does not enjoy cigar smoke. Tradition dictates that smokers always select their own cigar and not be handed one by the host. The host is also responsible for supplying the tools necessary to prepare, light, and smoke a cigar.

As a guest, you should select a cigar quickly and with appreciation. You do not fondle your host's collection. A host is always flattered if you ask him or her for a recommendation. When choosing a cigar, pick it up by its tuck, never by its head, as that is the end put into the mouth. Do not insult your host by overinspecting the cigar or by putting it to your ear to "listen to the band." If you have a cigar of your own that you'd rather smoke, hold it up to your host and ask if you may smoke it before seeing your host's selection. Refusing a host's cigar after reviewing his or her selection and then opting for your own is just plain rude.

If you have with you a cutter and lighter that you prefer to use, this is perfectly acceptable. It should go without saying that all cuttings, cellophane wrappers, matches, ashes, and other scraps from smoking should go into ashtrays or wastebaskets, not onto plates, glasses, or the floor or yard.

Perfect Pairing

Most cigar smokers don't smoke in public unless they feel certain that no one will be offended. You certainly can smoke without fear of offending at specially organized smoking events, at restaurants that allow cigar smoking, and in smoking clubs. A perfect companion to a good cigar is a cordial of brandy, port, or liquor.

Speaking of cordials, consider floating one in a snifter in a spa to warm it up while you enjoy a quiet, relaxing time with your husband or other special person. Light up your cigars, turn on the jets, and sit back. As cigar smoking is more and more becoming an outdoor activity, what better place to enjoy it than in the privacy of an intimate setting.

Location, Location, Location

When we're searching for a property, any realtor worth her car phone will emphasize the need to pay particular attention to where the property is located.

Likewise, women who appreciate a good cigar know that it's important to give some thought to where they enjoy smoking. Because they *are* worried that their smoking might offend someone, they pick places where that worry is eliminated.

Surely no woman—least of all Fidel Castro's maid—would approve of the place where he smokes his cigars. In Castro's opinion, "There is nothing more agreeable than having a place where one can throw on the floor as many cigar butts as one pleases without the subconscious fear of a maid who is waiting like a sentinel to place an ashtray where the ashes are going to fall." To those smokers who are inclined toward etiquette, it goes without saying: "Don't throw your cigar stubs on the floor."

So, where to smoke a good cigar? Consider:

- in a bubble bath
- while walking the dog
- while skimming the swimming pool
- in a wind-protected area on the deck of a cruise ship
- while lying in a hammock
- in front of a fire
- while walking in a new town that you've traveled to or in an unexplored area where you live
- while reading a novel in your favorite chair
- during a mother/adult son conference or a father/adult daughter conference (or a variation thereof)
- in an outdoor spa
- during an evening of window-shopping
- after a movie or a play

There are many little nooks and crannies that are often overlooked. Don't pass over places where the expe-

rience can be shared with a loved one or a friend. And
back to that vacation thing: How about a cigar while
soaking up the splendor of the Grand Canyon or sitting
on the edge of Rome's Trevi Fountain, or while viewing
the Alps from the top of the Matterhorn? The top of the
Eiffel Tower? The Top of the Mark? Enjoy!

Making a Memory

When you entertain or share your cigar-smoking experience, it's a considerate touch to provide something with
which to light the cigars. Before people had matches,
they used long, slender splinters of wood—sometimes
called *spills*—much as we use matches. Usually these
splinters were kept on the hearth of the fireplace and
ignited in the fire to light candles, oil lamps, pipes, and
cigars. In that tradition, the long, sulfur-free cedarwood
matches offer old-fashioned grace.

If you do use sulfur matches, let the sulfur burn off
before lighting a cigar. Don't use mechanical lighters
with a gasoline flame. Butane lighters are better.

Memories of special moments often are vividly
recalled when you hear certain songs or smell certain fragrances. You prefer that your memories be pleasant ones,
and lighted candles, placed in a room while you're smoking, not only provide ambiance but also help to dissem-
inate the afterodor of cigar smoke. The candles that you
choose should not be scented—their scent could com-
bine with cigar smoke to create an olfactory napalm.
Candles should never be used to light cigars. Their flame
contains wax, which could end up inside your cigar.

When the last cigar is extinguished, blow out the
candles, turn out the lights, and sleep secure in the
knowledge that you've done it right.

Odors Away

Cigar odor has always been a concern, especially for
women. But many products are available to rid your

home, car, and self of any lingering odor.

Baking soda is an easy and inexpensive solution. Place baking soda in any ashtray, and the odor will disappear. Baking soda also comes in a "freezer pack" that can be easily placed under car seats or in a room to absorb the odor. Be sure to change the baking soda regularly.

There are aerosol pump products that instantly remove odor with a single mist of spray. One that works particularly well is Bio Zapp. Such sprays can safely be used on clothing, carpeting, and furniture. They may also be sprayed into the return vents of air-conditioning systems, although these vents should be professionally cleaned to eliminate all odors.

Hand odor is a problem if you've allowed your hands to bathe in the smoke from your cigar. A product called Nonion is a piece of metal shaped like a bar of soap. Rubbing Nonion on your hands under water removes all odors.

CHAPTER 8

TRIVIA

This and That

The next time you light up with cigar-smoking friends, family, or a significant other and want to impress them, rattle off some of the following cigar miscellany. If anything, these tidbits are great conversation starters.

- Victor Muñoz, the famed journalist who established Mother's Day as a holiday, was once a reader to cigar rollers in Cuba.
- Sherlock Holmes was an expert on cigar ashes. He boasted of being able to identify any brand of cigar known to man by examining the ash.
- On December 9, 1983, a vintage collection of two hundred thousand Cuban cigars went on the auction block in New York City's 7th Regiment Armory. This was the first legal purchase of Cuban cigars in the United States since John F. Kennedy placed the embargo on them in 1962. The first lot of twenty-five sold for $2,100 to Al Goldstein, the publisher of *Screw* magazine.
- There's a five-year-old Thoroughbred racing horse named Cigar.
- When cigars are made, the filler's moisture content

is 16 percent. Binders and wrappers are 25 to 35 percent moisture. If the filler is too moist, it won't burn well and will prevent the smoker from getting a sufficient volume of smoke. Therefore, a cigar should be stored until all three components average 14 to 16 percent moisture before packaging.

- The CIA was alleged to have once contemplated assassinating Castro by getting him to unwittingly smoke an exploding cigar.

- Simon Argeritch, a cigar chain-smoker, holds the world record of seventeen for "most cigars held in the mouth and smoked simultaneously." He can whistle a tune at the same time.

- During the early 1600s, Italian, Spanish, and Austrian Catholic priests commonly smoked cigars while celebrating Mass.

- Tobacco leaves once were believed to have strong curative powers. They were placed on open wounds, running sores, even tumors. Chewing tobacco is said to prevent scurvy and gastric complaints.

- Bismarck, Germany's Iron Chancellor, praised the cigar's invaluable contribution to diplomacy. He even interrupted the peace negotiations that eventually ended the Franco-Prussian War to deliver a homily on the cigar's role in helping to bring about a just settlement.

- During espionage activities from 1914 to 1918, two German spies toured British ports posing as cigar merchants in order to observe Allied naval movements. Their reports read like orders for Havana cigars. Each cigar size corresponded to a particular class of warship. For example, an order for six hundred double coronas indicated that six battleships had been spotted at the port of consignment.

- Cellophane used to protect the cigar is highly flammable. The surgeon general therefore suggests that a cigar not be lighted until the cellophane is removed. (Makes sense.)

⬧ While choosing a cigar for her man in the movie *Gigi,* Leslie Caron held the cigar to her ear while rolling it between her finger and thumb. This procedure is known as "listening to the band" and is actually a worthwhile exercise. Put a cigar to your ear, roll it, and listen for crackling sounds. If you hear them, chances are the cigar is too dry.

⬧ A superstition holds that, when "ill will" is present, smoking a cigar will "clear the air."

⬧ A self-lighting cigar has been worked on for years with little success. Like a match, it lights when struck on the side of the packet. The exploding cigar came from this idea.

⬧ Hurricane Gilbert in 1988 wreaked havoc with the tobacco industry. In particular, it destroyed tobacco factories in Jamaica and Cuba.

⬧ Cigar ash mixed with camphorated chalk makes an excellent tooth powder. Ash ground with poppy oil makes a great oil-paint series of grays for a painter.

⬧ If all of the wrapper leaves on a tobacco plant are good, the plant can wrap thirty-two cigars.

⬧ In 1966 a German cigar manufacturer caused quite an uproar when he introduced a cigar series with

How to Blow Smoke Rings

What you need: a cigar with dense smoke and a location with no breeze.

1. Draw a thick puff of smoke into your mouth.

2. Make a large, unstrained "O" shape with your mouth (the same shape that you make when exclaiming "Oh!").

3. Put your tongue on the bottom of your mouth and back to block your throat passage.

4. Keeping your mouth open, move your tongue up slightly and "pop" your jaw to push a little smoke out of your mouth. A smoke ring should appear.

When learning to blow smoke rings, it is helpful to be around someone who can already do it. Be sure to exhale all the smoke from your mouth before breathing in.

With a little practice, you should have it mastered in no time.

bands showing portraits of Adenauer, Napoleon, and Adolf Hitler.

- Cigars were originally packaged in bundles covered with pigs' bladders containing a pod or two of vanilla to improve the odor.

- The professional smokers known as *caladores* do their taste testing only in the morning, smoke about one inch of a cigar, then refresh their palates with sugarless tea.

- The first cigar store Indian in America was carved in England and installed in front of a Boston tobacco shop in 1730.

- A bale of tobacco weighing about three hundred pounds sells for more than $1,000.

- The Spanish-American War began when a cigar butt blew up the battleship *Maine* in Havana in 1898. "Remember the *Maine!*" became the American battle cry.

- At the turn of the century, Cuba had 120 tobacco factories. Today there are only eight.

- Europeans used little black boys made of iron to advertise their cigar stores.

- The best year for cigar sales in the United States was 1964. Sales soared to almost nine billion.

- By the 1880s, cigar store Indians stood in front of nearly every cigar store in America. Each Indian held an upraised tomahawk in one hand, a bunch of cigars in the other.

- Winston Churchill was a cigarette smoker for years because he couldn't afford cigars. About the middle of World War II, Cuba gave him a gift of ten thousand top-quality cigars, which he had carefully inspected before smoking.

- In 1850 the *New York Times* stated that more money was spent every day on cigars than on bread.

- One of Napoleon III's marshals ordered gold-tipped cigars monogrammed with the imperial "N" at a cost of $120,000.

☞ The first reported instance of the English smoking a cigar was in 1586. Three English ship captains were seen "drinking" tobacco publicly in London using twisted leaves or "segars."

☞ Although Churchill didn't begin smoking cigars until later in life, he managed to smoke an estimated quarter of a million. Favorites were double coronas or Lonsdales of *maduro* leaf. In later years, his favorite was a Havana with a band bearing his likeness.

☞ In Groucho Marx's movies, his cigars were never lit.

☞ A devoted cigar-smoking Dutchman named Mynheer van Klaes left instructions in his will to have as many smokers in Holland as possible attend his funeral and smoke throughout the ceremony. His coffin was lined with cigar-box wood. Mourners were encouraged to scatter their tobacco ashes on the lid. Van Klaes's will provided for the mourners to receive packages of cigars annually.

☞ Mark Twain chain-smoked cigars—cheroots of indifferent quality.

☞ Good Samaritan Hospital in Phoenix, Arizona, has a "Resolving Through Sharing" program for grieving parents who have lost a newborn. The child's personal belongings are given to parents in a cigar box decorated by hospital volunteers.

☞ Patria Restaurant in New York City offers the "Cigar Dessert"—a chocolate mousse cake in the shape of a cigar, complete with sugar matches. Address: 250 Park Ave. S., New York, NY 10003; phone: (212) 777-6211.

☞ The first known appearance of tobacco in fine art was in a painting by Dutch artist William Buijtewech in 1611.

☞ The College of William and Mary was initially funded by a tax of one cent per pound on all tobacco exported from Virginia and Maryland.

☞ In colonial days, cured tobacco leaves were an acceptable form of currency, particularly in the

Chesapeake region. Passage for prospective wives from London to Jamestown was 120 pounds of Virginia leaf—then two pence per pound.

- One of the first illustrations of a man smoking appears in a relief on the walls of a Mayan temple in Palengue, Mexico, circa A. D. 300.

- Smoking was so trendy in seventeenth-century England that there were professors of the art of smoking.

- First car equipped with an ashtray was a four-cylinder Daimler limousine, custom built for King Ferdinand of Bulgaria in 1914.

- First automobile cigar lighter appeared on the dashboard of the 1923 Mercedes roadster.

- The match was invented in 1805.

- Largest properly smokable cigar was made by Henry Clay and called the Koh-i-Noor. Made before World War II for a maharajah, it was eighteen inches long, forty-seven ring gauge.

- Apple cores were once used to provide the humidity in a box of cigars.

- A first: In 1815 Michel Ney—a marshal in Napoleon's army—made this last request before he was executed for treason: to be allowed to smoke one final cigar.

- Smoking, early on, was thought to reduce feelings of hunger and to increase physical stamina.

- *Stogie* is the familiar term for the long, thin, inexpensive cigar that was favored by drivers of the Conestoga wagons and is now a generic term for any cigar. It also refers to a heavy, roughly made boot or shoe.

- John Quincy Adams and Ulysses S. Grant were cigar devotees.

- More than forty thousand tobacco seeds are contained in a single pod. One hundred thousand seeds are needed to fill a thimble.

- It takes at least four years of training for a cigar roller to become highly skilled.

- To some people in some places (such as Britain and countries that were British colonies), smoking a cigar with its band on is like wearing clothes with the price tag showing.

- It takes at least ten years to become a *torcedor*—maker—of the finest cigars.

- The term *guttersnipe* was given to children who scoured the gutters, taking cigar bands off discarded butts to redeem for prizes, such as a baseball glove for 150 bands.

- Vernon Dunhill, brother of Alfred Dunhill, founder of the Dunhill tobacco shops, created the first lighter that could be lit one-handed—by sliding the thumb across the roll bar.

- The Internet has a Usenet news group devoted to cigars. Its name: alt.smokers.cigars.

- America Online offers cigar information in its Wine & Dine Online forum.

Those Guys and Their Cigars

- George Burns put his cigar print in the cement in front of Grauman's Chinese Theater in Los Angeles. He prefers El Producto Queens.

- Raul Julia smoked cigars in bed—with his wife's permission.

- Sigmund Freud smoked twenty cigars a day—Don Pedros and Reina Cubans. Likewise, Orson Welles. His preference was Por Larranagas double coronas.

- Groucho Marx smoked Dunhill 410s.

- David Letterman smokes Romeo y Julietas and Punch Churchills.

- Robert DeNiro prefers extra-large Havanas.

- Jim Belushi smokes Cuban Bolivars, Cohibas, and Partagas.

- David Frost is inclined toward Romeo y Julieta #2s.

- Jack Nicholson smokes Cuban Romeo y Julietas, Cohiba Robustos, and Montecristos.

⊭ Ron Perlman favors H. Upmanns from the Dominican Republic, custom made for him—thirty-eight ring gauge and long.

Time Capsule

The following tidbits are not trivial, but they will supplement your encyclopedia of cigar information.

Stocking up

On the eve of the U.S. embargo of Cuba, President Kennedy asked then press secretary Pierre Salinger to obtain one thousand Petit Upmann cigars. When they had been procured, by the following day, Kennedy signed the decree forbidding Cuban products from being imported into the United States.

⊭ Machine-made cigars were introduced in 1920. This caused handmade production in the United States to fall from 90 percent in 1924 to 2 percent by the end of 1950.

⊭ Due to the embargo of Cuba by President John F. Kennedy in 1962, deposed cigar factory owners fled to other countries and started production with their original brand names. As a result, Romeo y Julieta, H. Upmann, Partagas, Punch, Hoyo de Monterrey, Sancho Panza, and others have double labels that are dissimilar to their Havana counterparts. The Cuban cigar industry has been nationalized under a state monopoly—Cubatabaco.

⊭ In the 1993 film *Scent of a Woman*, Al Pacino's character is having a final fling, doing and having the best in New York City before attempting to take his own life. He requests two Montecristo #1 cigars from the Dunhill Shop.

⊭ During World War I, French commander Marshal Foch would smoke a cigar on the eve of an offensive to sharpen his judgment for what lay ahead.

⊭ There are more than fifty species of tobacco, yet only two are of commercial significance today.

⊭ In 1975 the United States Trademark Office ruled

that expatriates who owned the names of cigars made in Cuba before the Cuban government nationalized the factories were the rightful owners of the names and could use them in the United States.

▷ Cuba standardized brands and sizes in 1979. Varieties went from about one thousand to about five hundred.

▷ Today the Dominican Republic produces 47 percent of the handmade cigars imported into the United States.

▷ Cigar sales in the United States had been declining until the last few years. In 1964 cigar sales peaked at nearly nine billion, coinciding with the surgeon general's report on smoking. By 1992 sales had dropped to about two billion, including about one hundred million imported premium cigars.

▷ Premium imports rose to 109 million in 1993, 125 million in 1994. The current back order of premium imported cigars totals twenty to twenty-five million. Six million Cuban cigars are purchased by Americans and stored outside the States annually. It is not known how many Cuban cigars are illegally brought into the United States. One estimate is 10 percent of Cuba's production.

▷ In 1995 tobacco prices increased by 25 percent, spurred by a dramatic increase in demand. When more farmers start growing tobacco, prices might decrease, but that's not expected by the industry.

Clinton Declines to Quit Cigar Smoking

In mid-August of 1995, President Clinton came down hard on the tobacco companies and proposed regulations to keep cigarettes away from teenagers. When asked if he would give up his occasional cigar, he said he would not. He went on to say, "I try to set a good example…I try never to do it where people see. I admitted that I did, I did do it when Captain [Scott] O'Grady was found [in Bosnia] because I was so happy. It was a form of celebration."

So there we have it. Cigar smoking is acceptable. Thank you, Mr. President!

☞ The cost of labor in the Dominican Republic will increase by 20 percent by the end of 1995. The government has instituted two 10 percent increases in the minimum wage for 1995.

Flavored Cigars

Brands	Flavors
Arango	vanilla
El Sublimado	fifty-year-old cognac
John T's	cappuccino
	Cafe Ole
	cherry cream
Ornellas	cognac
	vanilla

CHAPTER 9

ACCESSORIES

The Perfect Climate

Ah, the Caribbean, with its balmy temperatures of sixty-five to seventy degrees and humidity of 70 to 73 percent. It's a perfect environment for us as well as for our cigars. Cigars, like plants and people, do best in one particular environment and should be protected from extremes of temperature and humidity. Many cigar smokers have learned through years of frustration and disappointment that the first thing they should be concerned with after buying a cigar is storing it properly until they are ready to light it up.

Cigars, as a rule, should not be left out in the open for more than an hour (unless, of course, you live in the Caribbean). Cigars left in a box without humidification will not retain their moisture content for more than five days. Many cigars come packaged in cellophane wrappers. This is good temporary protection but should not be counted on for more than a few weeks. Sealed aluminum tubes keep cigars for years if the tubes have not been opened and if the temperature has not changed drastically.

Storage

A popular method of cigar storage is the humidor. A humidor is a hermetically sealed box, usually made of wood, with a device called a *hygrometer* that monitors humidity. Humidors come in a variety of sizes and with various price tags. As one shops for a humidor, remember that Spanish cedar is the wood preferred for the lining by cigar aficionados. Other cedars have more oil and give off a stronger aroma, which could overinfluence the cigars and ruin their delicately blended flavor. Cedar helps to prevent cigars from drying out and furthers the maturing process. Therefore, the cedar should always be unfinished. Humidors should be kept in a cool location away from direct sunlight, which could cause temperature changes. If the temperature is allowed to remain in the eighties for some time, the dormant larvae of the tobacco beetle could hatch, destroying your cigars with their voracious appetites. If cigars are stored at a temperature lower than sixty-five degrees, humidity must be raised to compensate.

If budget is a concern, an austere but totally workable alternative is a coffee can with a tightly sealed lid and a slightly damp sponge or cotton ball placed inside. Be sure that your source of dampness does not touch the cigars.

Small humidors are also available for travel. They are made of wood or hard leather to prevent the cigars from being crushed. There are even briefcases with a built-in minihumidor and compartments for accessories.

A wide variety of pocket- or purse-size cigar cases also is available. Again, they are made of leather or wood. Many have a "telescope" feature that allows cigars of almost any length to be carried, and some also have a built-in minihumidifier.

A note on leather containers: Be sure that the leather is good and thick to protect cigars from being disfigured. But also be sure that the leather is lined to prevent cigars from absorbing leathery aromas.

Polyethylene or other sealable plastic bags come in handy for temporary storage. A good tobacconist will always put single cigars into a sealed plastic bag for you to preserve them until you get home. If you need to use the bag for a longer time, spray the inside with a mist of water or place a slightly damp sponge in it but away from the cigars. If you want to use a damper sponge, be sure that the bag is not completely sealed to allow for some airflow. Otherwise, mold will form. In general, excess air in a bag should be expelled before sealing.

Controversy surrounds the storage of cigars in refrigerators and freezers. Opponents fear that cigars could become dehumidified or take on the flavor of last night's meat loaf. But cigars *can* be safely stored in a refrigerator or freezer, and this is a great solution when no room is left in your humidor. Place the cigars in an airtight plastic bag (if storing a box, place it in a bag as well) and remove the excess air. Frozen cigars will survive only if slowly returned to room temperature. Therefore, put them first in the refrigerator for at least twenty-four hours, then bring them out into room temperature for at least one hour or until they no longer feel cool to the touch. A cigar should be smoked only at room temperature.

Cellophane wrappers and other coverings should be removed before the cigars are placed in a humidor. Leaving the coverings on makes the inside of your humidor look less organized and less aesthetically pleasing. It is not a good idea to store cigars for more than eighteen months. Experts have detected deterioration of flavor in cigars after this time—even in those stored under perfect conditions. Unlike wine, cigars are perishable. Both cigars and what they're stored in should be well-conceived. Remember—they represent the smoker.

Restoration

Cigars that have lost their moisture have less flavor and aroma, are less mild, and flake off in the mouth. Excessive dryness also causes unraveling of the wrappers. If cigars are allowed to get too dry, they are difficult, if not impossible, to restore. But be of good cheer: If moisture can leave a cigar, most of the time it can also be returned.

Because cigars lose moisture slowly, they must also regain it slowly. Any quick-fix attempts will fail. If you have a humidor with a humidity regulator, place the dried cigars at the bottom of the humidor. In about five or six weeks move the cigars close to the regulator itself.

Another method is to place the dried cigars in a large plastic bag with a glass of water or a very moist sponge. The bag should not be completely sealed to allow for a little airflow. Rotate the cigars every few days for about three weeks. This is not an exact science, but you'll know when the cigars have returned to smokable condition by their slightly spongy feel and by the lack of a crackling sound when you "listen to the band."

If you have a friendly relationship with your tobacconist, he might revive your cigars for you in his humidifier. This is not a usual service, but many tobacconists do offer it, as well as cigar storage if you don't feel comfortable storing your own.

Don't expect your restored cigars necessarily to smoke and taste like ones that have been properly cared for. Dryness causes cigars to lose much of their bouquet.

Ashtrays and Cutters

Most cigarette ashtrays do not accommodate the girth or length of a cigar, but many outstanding cigar ashtrays are available. There are some made of onyx, marvelous Italian cut glass, crystal, and quality glass set in fine wood. Some have metal sculptures precariously aligned to hold your cigar horizontally. When a lit cigar is not being handheld, it needs an appropriate resting place so that it can lie flat, not have to sit uncomfortably on its end. Most cigar ashtrays, therefore, have an elongated shape with a long, wide groove in which to place the cigar. If not this shape, circular or square ashtrays will have grooves in the edges to hold the cigar securely without "squeezing" it.

Then there are cutters. The cutter is probably the most important accessory to carry if you smoke in public. Cutters come in many styles and shapes, in all qualities and price ranges. The best are made of precious metals and come with a leather carrying case. Keep your cutter clean and sharp. Remember that this accessory is commonly offered for use to other cigar smokers and can cause you embarrassment if a user does not get a clean cut.

The Lighter Side

There is a difference between lighters for cigars and cigarettes. A lighter for a cigar should feel good in the hand, fit your palm, and have some heft. Opening the lighter should be effortless. The cap should swing fully away from the body of the lighter to make the flame accessible.

The flame should be adjustable and fat, and the lighter should work in windy situations. The lighter should allow you to keep the top open easily while you light the cigar.

Avoid petrol lighters (they burn oil instead of gas). Their fumes can contaminate the cigar's taste. Likewise, never use a candle to light a cigar—the wax vapors can ruin the taste.

If you use a match to light a cigar, be sure to let the match burn for a few seconds after striking it to let chemicals in the match head burn off; otherwise it can cause a bad flavor. Wonderful sulfur-free cedarwood matches are made especially for cigars—they are extra long to provide the increased time needed to light a cigar. The guidelines for using lighters apply to using matches as well.

Using a match may be more elegant than using a lighter, but it's time consuming and requires more than one match—and more finesse.

Matches have long been the most elegant light for a cigar and are making a comeback. Special cigar matches made of cedarwood with special striking heads and extralong shafts are a sign to other cigar smokers that you are not a novice. These matches are made under many brands and can be bought in most fine tobacco shops. Two quick tips on matches: Wait a few seconds to allow the sulfur on the match head to burn off before lighting your cigar. And if you have only the traditional short matches, strike two simultaneously to create a fatter flame to more evenly light your cigar.

Cigarwear

Special clothing for cigar smoking was designed long ago. The English gentry would separate after dinner: the men retiring to one room to smoke, the women to another to share tea and conversation. The men would don smoking jackets and quilted smoking hats that resembled cropped-off fezzes with a tassel on top. These garments were worn to protect the men's hair and clothing from smoking odors. Today the fashion at a "smoker" is black tie, but wouldn't it be nice to bring back the traditional costume?

In Latin American countries, the *guayabera,* although worn as a business shirt, is favored for smoking.

Sitting Pretty

I would be remiss not to mention the all-important, broken-in, big and comfortable leather smoking chair. Tradition demands that, after dinner, smokers retire to their special chair, light up, sip cognac, and relax. This chair is a cigar smoker's sanctuary.

Comfortable leather chairs abound. In fact, many couples buy them in pairs so that they can sit side by side and discuss the day's events. The only rule for such chairs is that they be oversized, leather, and comfortable for hours.

Et Cetera

Some less common cigar accessories include:

- bowls in which to deposit the tobacco clippings cut from the head of cigars and the cellophane wrappers
- a smoker's logbook to chronicle cigar selections and opinions
- poles on which to display the bands removed from cigars

Book Browsing

Great additions to a library or coffee-table collection are books about cigars and the people who smoke them. However, there are only a very few. Tobacco stores have a larger selection than do bookstores, which rarely have even one.

The few books available catalog the different cigar brands, list "cigar friendly" establishments, rate cigars, give historical perspective, and depict the many cigar labels, bands, and boxes. However, many of these books were not recently written, and many are out of print. Used bookstores might be your best bet.

The good things in life are not discovered by accident. Hobbies that turn into passions cry out for those possessions that are unusual and beautiful. Apply this principle to your selection of cigars and the accessories that enhance them.

Cigar Publications and Videos

Magazines
> *Cigar Aficionado*
> (1-800-344-0763)
> *The Cigar Monthly*
> (1-310-576-0565)

Newsletter
> *Cigar of the Month Club*
> (1-800-700-7661)

Video
> *The Pursuit of Pleasure:*
> *The Cigar*
> (1-800-766-5375)

GLOSSARY

"A" Nickname for the legendary double corona Montecristo "A." Nine and a quarter inches long with a forty-seven ring gauge.

American flavor Cigars made from Virginia tobacco. Known for being sweet tasting.

Anilladora A woman who attaches the band to a cigar and then places it in the cigar box.

Banda volado Tobacco used for binder.

Belicoso A rather thick cigar with a ring gauge of fifty-two. Its length is five and a half inches, and it has a shaped head for easy clipping.

Biddies Small cigars of the East Indies.

Binder The tobacco leaf that wraps around the filler tobacco to keep it together before the wrapper leaf is rolled on.

Body The shaft of the cigar.

Boite nature (BN **for short)** A cedar box without labels, vistas (decorative lithographs), or edging paper.

Booking Folding the filler tobacco leaves in half, thus creating a "book" effect before covering them with a binder leaf.

Brownskin Another word for "cigar."

Buckeye Name given to small cigar companies. Usually family owned and operated.

Bunch Filler tobacco wrapped in binder tobacco before the wrapper leaf is rolled on.

Bunco A cigar from India that is about the size of your little finger and is wrapped in a banana leaf.

Bundle Twenty-five to fifty cigars sold bundled together with a silk ribbon.

Burros Tobacco leaves placed in large piles for fermentation.

Calibre A cigar's length and ring gauge.

Cameroon wrapper An expensive and popular wrapper leaf grown in Cameroon, Africa.

Canon A rolled cigar prior to having its tuck (foot) and head trimmed and finished.

Cap A piece of tobacco shaped, then placed over the head of the cigar to close the head. Part of the cap will be clipped off before smoking.

Capa Cuban for "wrapper." Means "cape" or "cloak."

Casa de tabaco A wooden hut in a tobacco field where the

leaves are hung up for their initial drying.

Chaveta The tool that a cigar roller uses. A flat, semicircular piece of metal (usually cut from old saw blades) with the convex side sharpened for use as a knife to trim the cigar. The flat surface is used as a roller to keep a cigar's ring gauge.

Cheroot Another word for "cigar."

Chico A slim cigar four to five inches long with a cut end.

Churchill A double corona about seven inches long with a forty-seven ring gauge.

Cigarillo A cylindrical roll made of shredded tobacco leaves, unlike a cigar that is made of whole tobacco leaves.

Cohiba The name given to the tobacco plant by the Taino Indians of Cuba and Haiti. Now the brand name of a Cuban cigar.

Corona The classic Havana cigar size. Straight body, about five and a half inches long, with a forty-two ring gauge and a rounded head. Also the name given to the top two leaves of the tobacco plant.

Criollos Harsh-tasting cigars smoked by Cuban locals.

Cromo A form of lithography used to embellish cigar boxes. This art form is native to Cuba.

Cubatabaco Government monopoly that controls the manufacture and sale of all Cuban cigars.

Cujes The pole on which tobacco leaves are hung for drying in the barn known as a *casa de tabaco.*

Culebra A cigar made up of two or three smaller cigars that are twisted together. Invented in the nineteenth century to prevent cigar factory workers from stealing cigars. Each day each worker was given three cigars, which were twisted together while still wet. This gave the cigars a distinctive shape. Only these cigars were allowed to leave the premises. Each cigar in a *culebra* should be smoked individually.

Curly head The finish on the head of a cigar that is created by tightly twisting the remaining wrapper leaf. The curly head can be found on several premium cigars.

Demitasse A very small cigar measuring four inches long with a thirty ring gauge. Also called a "lady finger" or "young lady." Many tobacco stores try to sell this size to women.

Despalilladora A woman who destems tobacco leaves.

Double binder Two binder leaves, one on top of the other, used when rolling a cigar. The two binders give the cigar extra firmness.

Double corona A cigar measuring almost eight inches long, with a forty-nine ring gauge.

Dry cigars American name for cigars that are made by the Dutch and Swiss and are not humidified.

Dutch flavor Cigars made with Indonesian tobacco leaves.

EMS (English market selection) A name given to a rich, brown wrapper color favored by British cigar smokers.

Escogedora A woman who sorts tobacco leaves by color. She must have a keen eye to differentiate more than sixty-four shades of leaves.

Escogida A Cuban festival held in the villages each year by the planters to choose and grade tobacco leaves before the leaves are purchased by factory representatives. Also the name given to the house or barn used for sorting tobacco leaves.

Fabrica The factory where cigars are rolled.

Fabuloso The name associated with the biggest cigar by any standard.

Figurado Any cigar not shaped like a cylinder, i.e., pyramid or *culebra*.

Fileteador A person who lines the cigar box with *cromos*.

Filler The leaves that form the body of a cigar and are surrounded by the binder leaf and then the wrapper leaf. These leaves provide much of a cigar's flavor.

Finca A Cuban tobacco farm.

Finished head A finish on the head of a cigar in which the wrapper leaf is trimmed in a way that allows the wrapper to continue, up and around, to form the cap, thus making the wrapper and cap from one piece.

Flat head A cigar whose head is flat rather than rounded.

Foot The end of the cigar that is lighted. The foot can be either cut or closed. Also called the "tuck" end.

Frog strip When the stem is stripped from a leaf of tobacco for filler, the leaf is left in one piece that resembles the underside of a frog.

Full cut Another name for a guillotine cut.

Fumar crudo Holding a cigar in the mouth for a few seconds before lighting it. Means "coarse smoking" and is considered bad form.

Galera The room in a cigar factory where cigars are rolled. Usually a very large room.

Gavilla A sheaf of tobacco leaves before arriving at the factory. Also the name given to a *torcedor*'s bunch of tobacco leaves for the day. Usually twenty-five wrapper leaves and enough filler and binder tobacco.

Goma A flavorless, odorless glue that dries without a trace and is used to finish the end of a wrapper leaf and to attach the cigar band.

Guarantee seal A green and white rectangular strip of paper placed on a box of Cuban cigars that proves the cigars' origin. This seal is widely copied by counterfeiters.

Guayabera A four-pocket shirt worn by cigar makers. Its long-sleeve version is considered formal enough to wear without a tie to weddings.

Guillotine A cigar cutter with a hole in which to place the head of the cigar and a straight blade to shear off the head in one clean motion. Also used by *torcedors* as a gauge to measure the length of each cigar and then to cut it to proper length.

Hand A group of similar leaves (approximately twenty) that are bundled together at the bottom of their stems.

Handmade Describes a cigar that has been bunched and rolled entirely by hand.

Handrolled Describes a wrapper that has been handrolled onto the cigar. Sometimes used interchangeably with *handmade*.

Havana A cigar made in Cuba from Cuban leaves.

Head The end of the cigar that is clipped and held in the mouth.

Hecho a mano Phrase found on cigar boxes. Means "handmade."

HTL (homogenized tobacco leaf) The product of mixing powdered tobacco with pure cellulose, fibers, and water to create pulp, which is pressed into sheets and then used as wrappers on many machine-made cigars.

Humidorean The person in the humidor at a Dunhill cigar shop.

Hygrometer A device that measures relative humidity.

Koh-i-Noor The biggest smokable cigar ever made. Made in Cuba by Henry Clay for a maharajah.

Lancet A cigar accessory designed to pierce a hole in the cap of a cigar.

Legero Filler tobacco that burns fast.

Lonsdale A round and tight cigar measuring six and a half inches long with a forty-two ring gauge. It is thinner than a corona, but fatter than a panatela.

Maduro A cigar with a brownish black wrapper. Also a name given to a cigar with a very strong tobacco.

Marble head Another name for the rounded head of a cigar.

Marrying A common phenomenon in which tobaccos transfer oils and aromas to one another. Different tobaccos in a cigar will marry, creating a blend.

Matting Coating the wrapper of a cigarillo with tobacco powder, thus giving it a more uniform appearance, even burn, and a whiter ash.

Moho azul The "blue mold disease." A mildew that destroyed the 1981 Cuban tobacco harvest.

Mulling Another word for fermentation—drying the leaves to bring them to their proper color.

Panatela A cigar with a straight, slim body, about four and a half inches long with a twenty-six ring gauge. Also spelled *panatella,* in Spanish it means "a piece of cake."

Parejo A cigar that has the same thickness from tip to tip and has both ends open. It means "even."

Perfecto A classic-shaped cigar that many cartoon characters smoke. A wide cigar that tapers toward both the foot and the head. For a time, it was considered the perfect shape for a Havana. Many times both ends need to be cut. Generally, a perfecto is four to five inches long.

Perilla A cigar tip that is perfectly rounded and cut and sealed with *goma.*

Plancha A bundle of five wrapper leaves, also called a "hand."

Plume Not to be mistaken for mold. Plume is the crystallization of tobacco oils that appears as a light grayish green dust on the wrapper of a cigar. It appears on cigars that have been aged in a humidor for a long time. To many, a cigar with plume has better flavor.

Popular Cigars made in Cuba for Cubans only. They are never exported and are not of superior quality.

Premium cigar Any handmade cigar with long filler leaves, high-grade tobacco, and a retail value of one dollar or more.

Puro A cigar whose filler, binder, and wrapper tobacco are all from the same origin. Also the Spanish name for "cigar."

Pyramid A cigar with a very wide foot that narrows to a smaller ring gauge.

Quebrado A tobacco leaf that has been broken or torn while in the field.

Ring gauge A system of measuring the diameter of a cigar. It uses an inch divided into sixty-four units. For example, a cigar with a thirty-two ring gauge is half an inch thick. A sixty-four ring gauge means the cigar has an inch diameter.

Rubio A pale cigar. *Rubio* means "blonde."

Rueda One hundred cigars packed together for sale.

Scrap filler The leftover tobacco cuttings used in the manufacturing of cigars. This is not short filler.

Seco Filler tobacco that burns slowly.

Semillero A nursery for tobacco seedlings.

Serone A large basket made of palm leaves and used to carry dried tobacco from the fields. Each *serone* carries roughly one hundred pounds.

Singles Cigars individually wrapped in cellophane, metal tubes, or cedar to protect them from moisture and damage.

Smoker A cigar-smoking event. Many times a smoker is an elaborate meal, with fine wines, at which dress is "black tie."

Spots Light yellow or greenish spots on a cigar caused by a reaction between the sun and moisture on the leaf. Spots in no way affect the quality of a cigar.

Stogie Slang term meaning any cigar. A shortening of *Conestoga,* referring to a region in Pennsylvania where early American cigars (and Conestoga wagons) were made.

Strength The strength of a cigar's smoke. It increases as the filler leaf gets darker.

Stripping Removing the stem of a tobacco leaf.

Taburete The leather stool that a *torcedor* sits on.

Tapado A tobacco field that has cheesecloth suspended over it to reduce the tobacco's exposure to the sun. Generally, wrapper leaves are grown using this technique so that the leaves will be light in color.

Tercio A sheaf of tobacco (called a *gavilla* before arriving at the factory) receiving treatment at the factory.

Tobacco The word may be an adaptation of the word *Tobago* (a Caribbean island) or of the word *Tabasco* (a province of Mexico).

Torcedor A master of the art of rolling cigars. It means "one who twists."

Torpedo A cigar whose shape widens from the head to the foot but then quickly narrows at the foot. Also called a "magnum." Its length is a little more than six inches.

Toscani An Italian cigar that is black, slim, and curved. It has very strong smoke.

Tuck The foot of a cigar.

Vega A tobacco plantation.

Veguero A person who plants, harvests, and monitors tobacco plants.

Vista A decorative lithograph placed on cigar boxes. Usually oval or rectangular.

Vitola Spanish word for the size and shape of a cigar.

Vitole A wooden board with holes drilled to certain ring gauges. As a quality control measure, cigars are passed through the holes to ensure consistency in sizing.

Vitolphile A collector of cigar bands.

Vuelta Abajo An area of Cuba that represents only 2 percent of Cuba's land but that, due in part to exceptional soil, produces the greatest tobacco in the world.

Whiff A Dutch-type cigar that is smaller than a cigarillo and cut on both ends.

Wrapper A cigar's outer leaf, which is rolled over the binder. The wrapper leaf is usually the finest tobacco available.

"Z" The seal of a Davidoff cigar. Zino Davidoff was the founder and owner.